The Lincoln Legion

DRAWN BY ARTHUR I. KELLER.

*"Now, sonny, you keep that pledge, and it will be the
best act of your life!"*

ABRAHAM LINCOLN PLEDGES CLEOPAS BRECKENRIDGE TO
TOTAL ABSTINENCE.

THE LINCOLN LEGION

The Story of
Its Founder and Forerunners

By

Rev. LOUIS ALBERT BANKS, D. D.

AUTHOR OF "THE HALL OF FAME," "THE YOUTH OF
FAMOUS AMERICANS," "HERO TALES FROM
SACRED STORY," "THE GREAT
PORTRAITS OF THE BIBLE,"
ETC., ETC.

Illustrated with Drawings by
ARTHUR I. KELLER
And Photographs

NEW YORK
THE MERSHON COMPANY
Presbyterian Building, 156 Fifth Ave.

AUTHOR'S PREFACE

THE reader of this volume needs to bear in mind the necessarily restricted scope of the book. The volume is intended to awaken interest in a new pledge-signing movement, and is, therefore, confined in its discussions to individuals, societies, and movements which have been peculiarly identified with urging total abstinence and fostering it through the pledge method. This accounts for many silences, such as that concerning the Hon. Neal Dow, the Nestor of Prohibitionists, and the long and noble list of eloquent and self-sacrificing orators and workers of the National Prohibition Party, and in other lines of temperance effort. We have treated at some length the Anti-Saloon League, because its Superintendent, Dr. Howard H. Russell, is the author of the new movement, and it is chiefly through the League, as representing all the churches, that the " Lincoln Legion " is to be carried forward.

LOUIS ALBERT BANKS.

NEW YORK CITY, *June* 23, 1903.

CONTENTS

ILLUSTRATIONS

9

LET US BUILD TO THIS TYPE

. . . Standing like a tower,
Our children shall behold his fame,
The kindly, brave, foreseeing man,
Sagacious, patient, dreading praise, not blame,
New birth of our new soil, the first American.
—JAMES RUSSELL LOWELL.

From the union of the colonists, Puritans and Cavaliers, from the straightening of their purposes and the crossing of their blood, slow perfecting through a century, came he who stands as the first typical American, the first who comprehended within himself all the strength and gentleness, all the majesty and grace of this republic—Abraham Lincoln.

He was the sum of Puritan and Cavalier, for in his ardent nature were fused the virtues of both, and in the depths of his great soul the faults of both were lost. He was greater than Puritan, greater than Cavalier, in that he was American.

Let us build with reverent hands to the type of this simple, but sublime life, in which all types are honored.—HENRY W. GRADY, *of Georgia. From his speech at the New England Club, New York, December 21, 1886.*

THE HEROIC YOUNG LINCOLN AS A TOTAL ABSTAINER

Let us have faith that right makes might, and in that faith as to the end, dare to do our duty.—ABRAHAM LINCOLN.

CHAPTER I

ABRAHAM LINCOLN was a child of the backwoods, when the frontiers of civilization were in Indiana and Illinois. At ten years of age he could handle an ax almost equal to a man, drive a team, manage a shovel-plow, wield the sickle, thresh wheat with a flail, fan and clean it with a sheet, and go to mill and take his turn with the grist. Even at that age, when his father did not need him, he was sent out to help the neighbors. His gaunt figure grew strong as iron, bearing the heavy loads under which it struggled.

Very early Lincoln got a thirst for reading. He had only chance enough at school to learn to read, and write, and " cipher to the rule of three." But he read the Bible,

Æsop's Fables, "Robinson Crusoe," Bunyan's "Pilgrim's Progress," Weems' "Life of Washington," and the "Statutes of Indiana." He read these until he almost knew them by heart, and then he searched the country around for other books to conquer, among them Shakespeare and Weems' "Life of Marion." He once told Leonard Swett that he had got hold of and read through every book he ever heard of in the part of the country where he lived for a circuit of fifty miles.

It is hard to-day to appreciate the emptiness and poverty of a life like Abraham Lincoln's boyhood, and the heroism that came off victorious over such conditions.

After he became President, one day at a Cabinet Meeting Lincoln said to Mr. Seward:

"Seward, did you ever hear how I earned my first dollar?"

"No," said Mr. Seward.

Well," replied he, "I was about

eighteen years of age, and belonged, as
you know, to what they call down South,
the 'scrubs'; people who do not own land
and slaves are nobody there; but we had
succeeded in raising, chiefly by my labor,
sufficient produce, as I thought, to justify
me in taking it down the river to sell.
After much persuasion I had got the consent of my mother to go, and had con-
structed a flat boat, large enough to take
the few barrels of things we had gathered
to New Orleans. A steamer was going
down the river. We have, you know, no
wharves on the Western streams, and the
custom was, if passengers were at any of
the landings, they were to go out in a boat,
the steamer stopping and taking them on
board. I was contemplating my new boat,
and wondering whether I could make it
stronger or improve it in any part, when
two men with trunks came down to the
shore in carriages, and looking at the different boats singled out mine, and asked,
'Who owns this?' I answered modestly 'I

do.' 'Will you,' said one of them, 'take us
and our trunks out to the steamer?' 'Certainly,' said I. I was very glad to have the
chance of earning something, and supposed that each of them would give me a
couple of bits. The trunks were put in my
boat. The passengers seated themselves
on them, and I sculled them out to the
steamer. They got on board, and I lifted
the trunks and put them on the deck. The
steamer was about to put on steam again,
when I called out, 'You have forgotten to
pay me.' Each of them took from his pocket
a silver half-dollar and threw it on the
bottom of my boat. I could scarcely believe my eyes, as I picked up the money.
You may think it was a very little thing,
and in these days it seems to me like a
trifle, but it was a most important incident in my life. I could scarcely credit
that I, the poor boy, had earned a dollar
in less than a day; that by honest work I
had earned a dollar. I was a more hopeful and thoughtful boy from that time."

From childhood, Abraham Lincoln had a gentle and tender nature. His stepmother, who came into the home when he was ten years of age, said of him after he was dead:

"Abe was a good boy, and I can say what scarcely one woman—a mother—can say in a thousand. Abe never gave me a cross word or look, and never refused, in fact or appearance, to do anything I requested him. I never gave him a cross word in all my life. His mind and mine— what little I had—seemed to run together. He was here after he was elected President. He was a dutiful son to me always. I think he loved me truly. I had a son, John, who was raised with Abe. Both were good boys, but I must say, both now being dead, that Abe was the best boy I ever saw, or expect to see."

Young Lincoln early developed a spirit of helpfulness toward the weak, or anyone or anything that was in trouble. The thoughtless cruelty to animals so common to children brought up among rude conditions, was never engaged in or enjoyed by him. While yet a boy he wrote essays on "Cruelty to Animals," and never failed to make his protest on seeing any dumb creature abused.

A striking instance of this kind and helpful spirit is referred to by several of his biographers. One evening, while returning from a "raising" in the neighborhood, with a number of companions, he discovered a straying horse, with saddle and bridle upon him. The horse was recognized as belonging to a man who was accustomed to excess in drink, and it was suspected at once that the owner was not far off. A short search only was necessary to confirm the suspicion of the young men. The poor drunkard was found in a perfectly helpless condition, upon the chilly ground. Abraham's companions urged the cowardly policy of leaving him to his fate, but young Lincoln would not listen to the proposition. At his request, the miserable sot was lifted to his shoulders, and he actually carried him eighty rods to the nearest house. Sending word to his father that he would not be back that night, with the reason for his absence, he attended and nursed the man until the morning, and had the pleasure of believing that he had saved his life.

When Lincoln was nineteen years of age he visited New Orleans in charge of a neighbor's flatboat, and while there witnessed a slave auction. Mr. Herndon says that he often heard Mr. Lincoln refer to this experience:

"In New Orleans for the first time," he writes, "Lincoln beheld the true horrors of human slavery. He saw negroes in chains —whipped, and scourged. Against this inhumanity his sense of right and justice rebelled, and his mind and conscience were awakened to a realization of what he had often heard and read. No doubt, as one of his companions has said, 'slavery ran the iron into him then and there.' One morning, in their rambles over the city, the trio passed a slave auction. A vigorous and comely mulatto girl was being sold. She underwent a thorough examination at the hands of the bidders; they pinched her flesh, and made her trot up and down the room like a horse, to show how she moved, and, in order, as the auctioneer said, that 'bidders might satisfy themselves whether the article they were offering to buy was sound or not.' The whole thing was so revolting that Lincoln moved away from the scene with a deep feeling of 'unconquerable hate.' Bidding his companions follow him, he said: 'Boys, let's get away from this. If I ever get a chance to hit that thing [meaning slavery], I'll hit it hard.' "

It is not possible for us to follow the story of this young and heroic figure through all his struggles as clerk in a country store, and surveyor's helper, always working against odds, always climbing to something better, always the manly youth, but constantly handicapped by poverty. His life-long friend, Joshua Speed, gives us a most lifelike portraiture of the beginning of Lincoln's career as a lawyer. He says:

" He had ridden into town on a borrowed horse, with no earthly property save a pair of saddle-bags containing a few clothes. I was a merchant at Springfield, and kept a large country store, embracing dry goods, groceries, hardware, books, medicines, bed-clothes, mattresses—in fact, everything that the country needed. Lincoln came into the store with his saddle-bags on his arm. He said he wanted to buy the furniture for a single bed. The mattress, blankets, sheets, coverlid, and pillow, according to the figures made by me, would cost seventeen dollars. He said that, perhaps, was cheap enough; but, small as the price was, he was unable to pay it. But if I would credit him till Christmas, and his experiment as a lawyer was a success, he would pay then; saying in the saddest tone, 'If I fail in this, I do not know that I can ever pay you.' As I looked up at him, I thought then, and I think now, that I never saw a sadder face.

" I said to him: ' You seem to be so much pained at contracting so small a debt, I think I can suggest a plan by which you can avoid the debt, and at the same time attain your end. I have a large room, with a double bed, upstairs, which you are very welcome to share with me.'

" ' Where is your room?' said he.

" ' Upstairs,' said I, pointing to a pair of winding stairs which led from the store to my room.

" He took his saddle-bags on his arm, went upstairs, set them on the floor, and came down with the most changed expression of countenance. Beaming with pleasure, he exclaimed:

" ' Well, Speed, I am moved.' "

Abraham Lincoln, throughout his life, boy and man, always stood for temperance. Far back in his Indiana boyhood, the first essay he ever wrote, was on the subject of Temperance. A local Baptist preacher was so struck with its merit that he secured it from the boy, and sent it to Ohio, where it is said to have appeared in a newspaper.

Soon after coming to Springfield to practice law, he joined the Sons of Temperance, and, as we shall see in the next chapters, frequently made temperance speeches, of very effective character.

The story is told by Judge Weldon that he was once in the room with Stephen A. Douglas when Lincoln entered. Douglas, desiring to show his hospitality, in accordance with the customs of the times, brought out a bottle of whisky, and some glasses, and invited his callers to take a drink with him. Lincoln respectfully declined on the ground that he had always been a temperance man, and felt that he was too old to change.

Leonard Swett tells us that Lincoln told him not more than a year before he was elected President that he had never tasted liquor in his life. "What!" said Swett, "do you mean to say that you never tasted it?" "Yes," replied Lincoln, "I never tasted it." When we take into consideration the habits of the time, this is a most remarkable testimony to Lincoln's temperance principles, the stability of his character, and the iron quality of his will-power.

Mr. C. C. Coffin, a most distinguished journalist of the day, who accompanied the notification committee from the Chicago Convention to Springfield, at the time of Lincoln's first nomination for the Presidency of the United States, related in his newspaper a few days later an incident that occurred on that occasion. He says that, after the exchange of formalities, Lincoln said:

" Mrs. Lincoln will be pleased to see you, gentlemen. You will find her in the other room. You must be thirsty after your long ride. You will find a pitcher of water in the library."

The newspaper man crossed the hall, and entered the library. There were miscellaneous books on the shelves, two globes, celestial and terrestrial, in the corners of the room, and a plain table, with writing materials upon it, a pitcher of cold water, and glasses, and no wines or liquors. There was humor in the invitation to take a glass of water, which was explained to Mr. Coffin by a citizen of Springfield, who said that, when it was known that the committee was coming, several citizens called upon Mr. Lincoln, and informed him that some entertainment must be provided.

" Yes, that is so. What ought to be done? Just let me know, and I will attend to it," he said.

" Oh, we will supply the needful liquors," said his friends.

" Gentlemen," said Mr. Lincoln, " I thank you for your kind attention, but must respectfully decline your offer. I have no liquors in my house, and have never been in the habit of entertaining my friends in that way. I cannot permit my friends to do for me what I will not myself do. I shall provide cold water—nothing else."

The Hon. John Hay, the present Secretary of State, and one of Lincoln's secre-

taries and biographers, has declared that
Lincoln was a man of extremely temperate
habits, and that he made no use of either
whisky or tobacco during all the years of
his association with him.

Mr. John G. Nicolay, his private secretary, and a joint biographer with Secretary
Hay, says: "During all the five years of
my service as his private secretary, I never
saw him drink a glass of whisky, and I never
knew or heard of his taking one."

From all this it will be seen that Abraham Lincoln, in his heroic struggle against
poverty and hard conditions, in his victory
over the vicious habits and customs of the
day in which he lived, in the fidelity to principle, and in the cleanliness and purity of
his personal habits of life, stands out before
us as an ideal leader of the new army of
total abstainers to which his name has been
given.

LINCOLN AT SOUTH FORK
SCHOOLHOUSE

In Lincoln there was always some quality that fastened him to the people, and taught them to keep time to the music of his heart.—David Swing.

CHAPTER II

THERE is in Springfield, Illinois, in Mr. Roland Diller's home, on Seventh Street, a legislative desk, which is notable because it is the desk which Abraham Lincoln used when he was a member of the Legislature, between 1830 and 1840. The desk is an interesting relic, also, because it shows the primitive furniture of the Illinois State Capitol of those days. His biographers have noticed it was Mr. Lincoln's habit to write his name upon books, papers, and other belongings, and, following that practice, Lincoln left his autograph heavily marked with a lead pencil inside the drawer of this desk, so that, to this day, any student of autographs easily recognizes Lincoln's unique handwriting. This, with abundant other evidence, identifies beyond question

29

the desk as actually having been the one used by Mr. Lincoln.

Early in 1900, Dr. Howard Russell, the Superintendent of the Anti-Saloon League, visited Diller's drug store in Springfield, where the desk then stood, to look at this relic of the great war President. Mr. Diller gave Russell many interesting facts regarding Lincoln. Diller was born in 1822, so he is now an old man, eighty-one years of age. He lives on the next corner, a block away from Mr. Lincoln's home, and has lived there since 1844. He was not only a neighbor, but an intimate friend of Mr. Lincoln, and his drug store was one of Mr. Lincoln's favorite haunts, where politics were discussed and stories told. When Dr. Russell told Diller of the Temperance Reform work in which he was engaged, the druggist told him that Mr. Lincoln, from the time Diller first knew him in 1844, to the time of his death, was always a most pronounced temperance man; that he never used intoxicating liquor in any form, and that he was most earnest and active in connection with the various reform movements of his day.

During this conversation, Mr. Diller informed Russell of an incident that left a very strong impression on Russell's mind. He said there was living in Sangamon County a farmer named Cleopas Breckenridge. This Mr. Breckenridge, Diller said, had a most interesting personal reminiscence concerning Abraham Lincoln, which had never been printed, and though he lived sixteen miles from Springfield, Diller was sure that Mr. Breckenridge was so enthusiastic a temperance man that he would be glad to meet the Superintendent of the Anti-Saloon League some time in Springfield, and personally state the facts to him.

A few months later, Dr. Russell, finding that he was going to be in Springfield on a certain day, wrote Mr. Diller and asked him to communicate with Mr. Breckenridge, and request him, if possible, to meet him there that day, and to inform him of the purpose for which he wished to see him. Sure enough, Breckenridge drove sixteen miles upon a stormy day, and met Russell as arranged at the Leland Hotel in Springfield, where he told him the following story, which now for the first time sees the publicity of print:

"When I was a boy," said Breckenridge, "about ten years of age, in the summer of 1846 or 1847, I lived with my father upon the same farm which I now own in Cotton Hill township in this county. We were very poor. My father was above the average in intelligence, but he had a large family, and was in debt, so that while we had enough to eat, we lived very plainly. My mother had died a short time before I was ten years old, and my father in those days was doing the best he could to be father and mother both to us children. One day, in the summer of 1846 or 1847, my father came home, and told us that there would be a temperance meeting held at the new schoolhouse, and that we could all go to the meeting if we wished to do so. Most of the family attended the meeting, though I believe my older brother Alexander was away from home, and did not go. The schoolhouse had been recently built, and the boughs of the trees from which the logs had been cut to build the house were scattered about on the ground in front of the house, and there were also some logs which had not been used in the building, lying about upon the ground. Some trees had been left for a shade, and as the day was warm, the meeting was held under the trees instead of in the schoolhouse. The people sat about on the boughs of the trees, and upon the logs. The speaker on the occasion was a young lawyer from Springfield who already had gained a reputation as a public speaker, and the announcement of the fact that he was to speak, called out a large crowd, almost all the families in that part of the county being represented.

" The speaker made a very earnest appeal for total abstinence from the use of all intoxicating drinks. He gave reasons why he was in favor of total abstinence, and why he thought others should become total abstainers. About the time he finished his address, he took a paper out of his pocket. 'This,' said he, 'is what is called the 'Washingtonian Pledge! It is the same pledge many thousands of people have signed in connection with the work of the Washingtonian Society throughout the country. I have signed this pledge myself and would be glad to have as many of my neighbors who are willing to do so, sign the same pledge with me.' The pledge was passed from one to another and was signed by a good many of those present. After a number had signed, the first thing I knew the speaker was standing in front of me. He said to me: 'Sonny, don't you want your name on this pledge?' I said: 'Yes, sir.' He said: 'You know what it means, that you are not to drink intoxicating liquor?' I said: 'Yes, sir.' He asked me my name and I told him, Cleopas Breckenridge. He wrote my name upon the paper, then he transferred the pencil to his left hand, and holding the paper and pencil in his left hand, he leaned over and laid his right hand upon my head and said: ' Now, Sonny, you keep that pledge, and it will be the best act of your life.' THE SPEAKER WHO ADDRESSED THAT MEETING, AND WHO WROTE MY NAME UPON THE PLEDGE, WAS ABRAHAM LINCOLN."

Dr. Russell asked Breckenridge what made him sure that the speaker was Abraham Lincoln. He replied that from time to time afterwards, he often saw Mr. Lincoln at Springfield, and at other places in Sangamon County, that he frequently heard him speak, and that on several occasions he was present when Mr. Lincoln entertained a crowd about him by conversation and stories. He said also that Mr. Lincoln on numerous occasions attended to law business for his father, Preston Breckenridge, and that it was his father's influence and invitation together with the request of other neighbors, that caused Mr. Lincoln to come and address the meeting at the schoolhouse that day. Russell asked Mr. Breckenridge why Lincoln signed the pledge for him. He said he could not write his name at that time. Mr. Lincoln did not ask him whether he could write his name or not, but knowing that boys of his age were usually unable to write at that period, Lincoln signed his name for him. Mr. Breckenridge then continued his story as follows:

"I felt that I was under solemn obligation to keep the pledge which Mr. Lincoln had signed for me, and I did keep it and have kept it up to the present time. In the year 1857, when I was twenty-one years of age, I went to Colorado and kept a tavern there for two years upon the trail across the plains at a point about fifty miles east of Denver. Friends advised me to buy a barrel of whisky and mix with it a barrel of river water and sell the liquor and make some money, but I said: ' No, I never drink it and I will not sell it,' and mine was the only temperance tavern that I ever heard of

DRAWN BY ARTHUR I. KELLER.

ABRAHAM LINCOLN'S APPEAL FOR TOTAL ABSTINENCE

At South Fork Schoolhouse, Sangamon County, Illinois, in 1847.

on the route across the plains. I returned
in about two years to Illinois, and when the
Civil War broke out enlisted in Company
D of the 33d Illinois Volunteer Infantry,
and one other man in the company, William
George, and I, were the only men I knew of
who did not drink, more or less. George
and I had extra guard duty and other services to perform because the other members
of the company were disabled and sick to a
large extent as the result of their drinking
habits. Several times when we were in
swampy or malarious territory in the South,
rations of whisky were served to the men,
but I always abstained from drinking it. I
was dangerously wounded at the siege of
Vicksburg, and while I was sick, my captain, thinking to do me a service, at con-
siderable trouble and a good deal of expense,
procured a bottle of brandy and brought it
to me at the hospital. I was sorry to hurt
his feelings, but was so determined not to
touch liquor, that in as kind a way as I
could, I explained the matter and refused

the brandy. He said: ' Why, this is simply for medicine, this will not violate your pledge '; but I told him I thought I would be as well off without it, and I would rather not drink any of it. After nearly four years' service I returned home and went to work on the farm, paid off the indebtedness and added more land to the original farm. My children are married and are living near me and I am spending a very happy life among my children and grandchildren. I believe the pledge which I made when I was a boy, as I have stated, and the fact that I have faithfully observed it, has been one of the essential elements in the success of my life."

Dr. Russell was so impressed with the remarkable story told by Mr. Breckenridge that in May, 1903, having business in that part of Illinois, he resolved that while there he would call at the home of Breckenridge, and on May 8th went out on the train from Springfield to Breckenridge Station. Both the station and the post office in the com-

munity were named after Preston Breckenridge, the father of Cleopas Breckenridge.
From there he drove two and one-half miles
to the Breckenridge farm, and was hos-
pitably received and entertained over night.
Mr. Breckenridge has a very thriving farm,
with a large two-story house upon it,
with well-equipped barns and all the com-
forts and conveniences of a modern well-to-
do farmer.   Among other things Dr. Russell saw, was the old log-house, still pre-
served, and used as a granary, in which Mr.
Breckenridge was born, and in which he
lived at the time he signed the pledge.   Russell asked Breckenridge during this visit if
he could tell him the names of any other persons still living who were present at the
Lincoln temperance meeting at the South
Fork Schoolhouse.   He could not at first
give him any names.   He said all of the old
neighbors had either died or moved away,
and much of the land of the neighborhood
was now being rented to new tenants.   The
next morning, however, before Russell left,

the old farmer recalled two men living at
Edinburg, twelve miles away, in the next
county, named Moses Martin and R. E.
Berry. He said these men lived in the
neighborhood at that time, and it was possible, and even probable, that they were present at the meeting.

Russell was now hot on the scent, and did
not let the trail grow cold. Saturday, May
9, 1903, he went to Edinburg. He had the
good fortune to find both the men that day,
and when he told them his errand, each
stated at once that he remembered the meeting, that he was present, and signed the
pledge at that meeting, and each has kept it
ever since. Russell asked if they were willing to make affidavit to the fact, and they
cheerfully assented. Mr. Cleopas Breckenridge also made affidavit to the story herein
related, but as the substance of it is already
told, it is omitted. But I am sure that
every reader will be interested in the affi-
davits of R. E. Berry and Moses Martin
which follow:

AFFIDAVIT OF R. E. BERRY.

State of Illinois
Christian County
   ss:

I, R. E. Berry, being duly sworn on oath, depose and say, that I am 79 years old and a resident of Edinburg, Christian County, Illinois.

That in 1841, at the age of 18, I worked for a time on the farm of Timothy Driscoll in Cotton Hill Township, Sangamon County, Illinois, which joined the farm of Preston Breckenridge on the east. That about 1851 I bought the said Driscoll farm and lived there until 1857, and then bought another farm upon which the present post office and railway station of Berry is situated. The post office was established while I owned the farm and I was postmaster until I left the farm in 1881.

In the years 1846 and 1847 I was making my home one and one-half miles east of the South Fork log schoolhouse. This schoolhouse was located on the west side of the road, across from the South Fork Christian Church, still in use as a church. I remember the Washingtonian Movement and the fact that pledge-signing meetings were held in various localities addressed by different speakers from Springfield and elsewhere. Among others who took part as speakers were John Webber and Preston Brecken-ridge, and among others Abraham Lincoln spoke at various places, from time to time.

I well remember the meeting that was held, and which I attended, one summer afternoon at the South Fork Schoolhouse. It was soon after the schoolhouse was built, and the tops of the trees from which the logs for the house were cut were lying about near the door of the house. The meeting was held out of doors; quite a congregation of men, women, and children were present, and they sat about on the limbs of the trees and logs which strewed the ground. The speaker was Abraham Lincoln, and after a very earnest speech in which he explained the Washingtonian Movement, and in which he advocated that all should sign and keep the pledge of total abstinence from in-toxicating liquors, he presented the pledge and asked for signers. I signed the pledge in that meeting and have kept the same to this day, and I have never regretted that I did so..

R. E. BERRY.

Subscribed and sworn to before me this 9th day of May, A. D., 1903, at Edinburg, Christian Co., Illinois.

B. A. TURNER,
Notary Public.

AFFIDAVIT OF MOSES MARTIN.

State of Illinois
Christian County
ss:

Moses Martin, of Edinburg, Christian County, Illinois, being duly sworn, on oath deposes and says, that he was seventy-five years old February 28, 1903. That he was born in Lawrence County, Indiana, and came with his father to Sangamon County, Illinois, late in the year 1830, and settled on a farm one mile south of what is now Breckenridge post office and station, and about three miles east of what is now known as the South Fork Christian Church. The South Fork Schoolhouse was built about

1846, across the road from the South Fork
Church aforesaid. I lived on the above-
mentioned farm from 1830 to 1867, and am
familiar with what transpired in the neighborhood during that period. In 1867 I went
to near Butler, Missouri, and in 1883 to
near Howard, South Dakota, and in 1893 I
returned to Sangamon County, Illinois, and
settled on the same farm formerly owned by
my father south of Breckenridge, as above
stated, which farm I still own, and I have
lived there until about one year ago, when
I removed to Edinburg.

I became interested in the Washingtonian
Temperance Movement in 1846. The first
meeting of the kind I ever heard of was
announced to be held at the new schoolhouse—the South Fork Schoolhouse—in the
summer or fall of that year. The meeting
was held in the open air near the schoolhouse, the people sitting upon the boughs of
trees and logs which had been cut when the
house was built. It had been announced
that Abraham Lincoln would speak and a
large crowd attended the meeting. Mr.
Lincoln made a very plain, earnest speech in
favor of total abstinence from all intoxicating liquors as beverages, and after his

speech he took a paper from his pocket and read a pledge which I afterward committed to memory from a copy made from the pledge read by Mr. Lincoln. It was as follows:

" THE WASHINGTONIAN PLEDGE.

" Whereas, the use of alcoholic liquors as a beverage is productive of pauperism, degradation, and crime and believing it is our duty to discourage that which produces more evil than good, we therefore pledge ourselves to abstain from the use of intoxicating liquors as a beverage."

Among those who signed the pledge in that meeting were George, William, and Uriah Hughes and their mother; Preston Breckenridge and his children, and R. E. Berry, now of Edinburg, Ills. I myself signed then and there—my first pledge— and I have kept it until now.

I further remember and state that after Mr. Lincoln had spoken and the pledge had been signed, Mr. Lincoln asked if anyone had anything to say for or against the movement, and Mr. Preston Breckenridge rose up and spoke of the importance of parents

taking an interest in the matter. The wife
of the said Breckenridge had recently died,
and he pointed to his motherless children
and spoke of his anxiety for them, and as he
spoke the tears ran down his face.

Afterward at various times and places the
said Preston Breckenridge held Washingtonian meetings and I went with him and
acted as secretary and helped enroll the
signers to the pledge.

The meeting above referred to conducted
and addressed by Abraham Lincoln was the
beginning of a series of Washingtonian
meetings which did great and lasting good
in this section of the country.

MOSES MARTIN.

Subscribed in my presence and
sworn to before me by Moses Martin of this village of Edinburg, this
11th day of May, A. D., 1903.

B. A. TURNER,
Notary Public.

Since these interesting testimonies were
given, and since Superintendent Russell's
return to New York, a letter has come from
Mr. Cleopas Breckenridge stating that he

has seen Mrs. Almarinda Bell Galloway, an old lady who lived in that neighborhood in her childhood, and she, too, states that she was present at the Lincoln meeting, and remembers it well.

Mr. Breckenridge also promised to invite the others to meet him at Springfield for a " reunion " of the survivors of the South Fork Lincoln meeting, and to have a photograph taken for this volume, and the picture has been received just in time for insertion opposite page 21.

ABRAHAM LINCOLN AS A TEMPER-
ANCE ORATOR

In relation to the principle that all men are created equal let it be as nearly reached as we can. If we cannot give freedom to every creature, let us do nothing that will impose slavery upon any other creature.— Abraham Lincoln.

CHAPTER III

ABRAHAM LINCOLN AS A TEMPERANCE ORATOR

ON Washington's Birthday, February 22, 1842, Abraham Lincoln delivered in Springfield, Illinois, before the Washingtonian Temperance Society a very remarkable address. This address, with the heading as given below, was printed on the first page of the Sangamon *Weekly Journal* in the issue of March 26, 1842. It is in the bound copy of the files of that journal. The copy for this chapter was made for this volume directly from the Sangamon *Weekly Journal* files, and afterward compared with the original. The italics used here are the very words which were underscored by Abraham Lincoln himself in preparing his manuscript for the occasion. The address in full is as follows:

AN ADDRESS,

Delivered before the Springfield Washingtonian Temperance Society, on the
22nd February, 1842,—
By ABRAHAM LINCOLN, Esq.,
And published by direction of the Society.

Although the temperance cause has been
in progress for near twenty years, it is ap-
parent to all, that it is, *just now*, being
crowned with a degree of success hitherto
unparalleled.

The list of its friends is daily swelled by
the additions of fifties, of hundreds, and of
thousands. The cause itself seems suddenly
transformed from a cold abstract theory, to
a living, breathing, active, and powerful
chieftain, going forth " conquering and to
conquer." The citadels of his great adver-
sary are daily being stormed and dis-
mantled; his temples and his altars, where
the rites of his idolatrous worship have long
been performed, and where human sacrifices

have long been wont to be made, are daily
desecrated and deserted. The trump of the
conqueror's fame is sounding from hill to
hill, from sea to sea, and from land to land,
and calling millions to his standard at a
blast.

For this new and splendid success, we
heartily rejoice. That that success is so
much greater *now* than *heretoforo*, is doubtless owing to rational causes; and if we
would have it to continue, we shall do well
to inquire what those causes are. The war-
fare heretofore waged against the demon of
intemperance, has, somehow or other, been
erroneous. Either the champions engaged,
or the tactics they adopted, have not been
the most proper. These champions for the
most part, have been preachers, lawyers,
and hired agents. Between these and the
mass of mankind, there is a want of ap-
proachability, if the term be admissible,
partially, at least, fatal to their success.
They are supposed to have no sympathy of
feeling or interest, with those very persons

whom it is their object to convince and persuade.

And again, it is so easy and so common to ascribe motives to men of these classes, other than those they profess to act upon. The *preacher,* it is said, advocates temperance because he is a fanatic, and desires a union of Church and State; the *lawyer,* from his pride and vanity of hearing himself speak; and the *hired agent,* for his salary. But when one, who has long been known as a victim of intemperance, bursts the fetters that have bound him, and appears before his neighbors " clothed, and in his right mind," a redeemed specimen of long lost humanity, and stands up with tears of joy trembling in his eyes, to tell of the miseries *once* endured, *now* to be endured no more forever; of his once naked and starving children, now clad and fed comfortably; of a wife, long weighed down with woe, weeping, and a broken heart, now restored to health, happiness, and renewed affection; and how easily it all is done, once it is resolved to be done; however simple his language, there is a logic, and an eloquence in it, that few, with human feelings, can resist. They cannot say that *he* desires a union of Church and State, for he is not a church member; they cannot say that *he* is vain of hearing himself speak, for his whole demeanor shows, he would gladly avoid speaking at all; they cannot say *he* speaks for pay, for he receives none, and asks for none. Nor can his sincerity in any way be doubted, or his sympathy for those he would persuade to imitate his example, be denied.

In my judgment, it is to the battles of this new class of champions that our late success is greatly, perhaps chiefly, owing.— But, had the old school champions themselves been of the most wise selecting, was their *system* of tactics, the most judicious? It seems to me, it was not. Too much denunciation against dram sellers and dram drinkers was indulged in. This, I think, was both impolitic and unjust. It was *impolitic*, because, it is not much in the nature of man to be driven to anything; still less to be driven about that which is exclusively his own business; and least of all, where such driving is to be submitted to, at the expense of pecuniary interest, or burning appetite. When the dram seller and the drinker, were incessantly told, not in the accents of entreaty and persuasion, diffidently addressed by erring men to an erring brother; but in the thundering tones of anathema and denunciation, with which the lordly judge often groups together all the crimes of the felon's life and thrusts them in his face just ere he passes sentence of death upon him, that *they* were the authors of all the vice, and misery and crime in the land; that *they* were the manufacturers and material of all the thieves and robbers and murderers that infested the earth; that *their* houses were the workshops of the devil; and that *their persons* should be shunned by all the good and virtuous, as moral pestilences,—I say, when they were told all this, and in this way, it is not wonderful that they were slow, *very slow,* to acknowledge the truth of such denunciations, and to join the ranks of their denouncers, in a hue and cry against themselves.

To have expected them to do otherwise than as they did—to have expected them not to meet denunciation with denunciation, crimination with crimination, anathema with anathema, was to expect a reversal of human nature, which is God's decree, and never can be reversed. When the conduct of men is designed to be influenced, *persuasion,* kind, unassuming persuasion, should ever be adopted. It is an old and a true maxim, that a " drop of honey catches more flies than a gallon of gall."—So with men. If you would win a man to your cause, *first* convince him that you are his sincere friend. Therein is a drop of honey that catches his heart, which, say what he will, is the great high road to his reason, and which, when once gained, you will find but little trouble in convincing his judg-

ment of the justice of your cause, if indeed
that cause really be a just one. On the
contrary, assume to dictate to his judgment,
or to command his action, or to mark him
as one to be shunned and despised, and he
will retreat within himself, close all the
avenues to his head and heart; and though
your cause be naked truth itself, transformed to the heaviest lance, harder than
steel, and sharper than steel can be made,
and though you throw it with more than
Herculean force and precision, you shall no
more be able to pierce him, than to pene-
trate the hard shell of a tortoise with a rye
straw.

Such is man, and so *must* he be understood by those who would lead him, even to
his own best interest.

On this point, the Washingtonians
greatly excel the temperance advocates of
former times. Those whom *they* desire to
convince and persuade, are their old friends
and companions. They know they are not
demons, nor even the worst of men. *They*

know that generally, they are kind, generous and charitable, even beyond the example of their more staid and sober neighbors. *They* are practical philanthropists; and *they* glow with a generous and brotherly zeal, that mere theorizers are incapable of feeling.—Benevolence and charity possess *their* hearts entirely; and out of the abundance of their hearts, their tongues give utterance. " Love through all their actions runs, and all their words are mild." In this spirit they speak and act, and in the same, they are heard and regarded. And when such is the temper of the advocate, and such of the audience, no good cause can be unsuccessful.

But I have said that denunciations against dram sellers and dram drinkers, are *unjust* as well as impolitic. Let us see.

I have not inquired at what period of time the use of intoxicating drinks commenced; nor is it important to know. It is sufficient that to all of us who now inhabit the world, the practice of drinking them, is just as old as the world itself,—that is, we have seen the one, just as long as we have seen the other. When all such of us, as have now reached the years of maturity, first opened our eyes upon the stage of existence, we found intoxicating liquor, recognized by everybody, used by everybody, and repudiated by nobody. It commonly entered into the first draught of the infant, and the last draught of the dying man. From the sideboard of the parson, down to the ragged pocket of the houseless loafer, it was constantly found. Physicians prescribed it in this, that, and the other disease. Government provided it for its soldiers and sailors; and to have a rolling or raising, a husking or hoe-down, anywhere without it, was positively insufferable.

So too, it was everywhere a respectable article of manufacture and of merchandise. The making of it was regarded as an honorable livelihood; and he who could make most, was the most enterprising and respectable. Large and small manufactories of it

ABRAHAM LINCOLN

As he appeared at the time of the Washingtonian Movement.

were everywhere erected, in which all the earthly goods of their owners were invested. Wagons drew it from town to town—boats bore it from clime to clime, and the winds wafted it from nation to nation; and merchants bought and sold it, by wholesale and by retail, with precisely the same feelings, on the part of seller, buyer, and bystander, as are felt at the selling and buying of flour, beef, bacon, or any other of the real necessaries of life. Universal public opinion not only tolerated, but recognized and adopted its use.

It is true, that even *then*, it was known and acknowledged that many were greatly injured by it; but none seemed to think that the injury arose from the use of a *bad thing*, but from the abuse of a *very good thing.*— The victims to it were pitied, and compassionated, just as now are, heirs of consumptions, and other hereditary diseases. Their failing was treated as a *misfortune*, and not as a *crime*, or even as a *disgrace*.

If, then, what I have been saying be true,

is it wonderful that *some* should think and act *now,* as *all* thought and acted *twenty years ago?* And is it *just* to assail, condemn, or despise them, for doing so? The universal *sense* of mankind on any subject, is an argument, or at least an *influence,* not easily overcome. The success of the argument in favor of the existence of an overruling Providence, mainly depends upon that sense; and men ought not, in justice, to be denounced for yielding to it, in any case, or for giving it up slowly, especially, where they are backed by interest, fixed habits, or burning appetites.

Another error, it seems to me, into which the old reformers fell, was, the position that all habitual drunkards were utterly incorrigible, and therefore, must be turned adrift, and damned without remedy, in order that the grace of temperance might abound to the temperate *then,* and to all mankind some hundred years thereafter.—There is in this something so repugnant to humanity, so uncharitable, so cold-blooded and feelingless, that it never did, nor ever can enlist the enthusiasm of a popular cause. We could not love the man who taught it—we could not hear him with patience. The heart could not throw open its portals to it. The generous man could not adopt it. It could not mix with his blood. It looked so fiendly selfish, so like throwing fathers and brothers overboard, to lighten the boat for our security—that the noble-minded shrank from the manifest meanness of the thing.

And besides this, the benefits of a reformation to be affected by such a system, were too remote in point of time, to warmly engage many in its behalf. Few can be induced to labor exclusively for posterity; and none will do it enthusiastically. Posterity has done nothing for us; and theorize on it as we may, practically we shall do very little for it, unless we are made to think, we are, at the same time, doing something for ourselves. What an ignorance of human nature does it exhibit, to ask or expect a whole community to rise up and

labor for the *temporal* happiness of *others*
after *themselves* shall be consigned to the
dust, a majority of which community take
no pains whatever to secure their own
eternal welfare, at a no greater distant day?
Great distance, in either time or space, has
wonderful power to lull and render quies-
cent the human mind.   Pleasures to be enjoyed, or pains to be endured, after we shall
be dead and gone, are but little regarded,
even in our *own* cases, and much less in the
case of others.

Still, in addition to this there is something so ludicrous in *promises* of good, or
threats of evil, a great way off, as to render
the whole subject with which they are connected, easily turned into ridicule. " Better
lay down that spade you're stealing, Paddy,
—if you don't you will pay for it at the day
of judgment."   " By the powers, if you'll
credit me so long, I'll take another, jist."

By the Washingtonians, this system of
consigning the habitual drunkard to hope-
less ruin, is repudiated.   *They* adopt a more

enlarged philanthropy. *They* go for present
as well as future good. *They* labor for all
now living, as well as all hereafter to live.—
They teach hope to all—despair to none.
As applied to *their* cause, *they* deny the doctrine of unpardonable sin. As in Chris-
tianity it is taught, so in this they teach,
that

> " While the lamp holds out to burn,
> The vilest sinner may return."

And, what is a matter of the most pro-
found gratulation, they, by experiment upon
experiment, and example upon example,
prove the maxim to be no less true in the
one case than in the other. On every hand
we behold those, who but yesterday, were
the chief of sinners, now the chief apostles
of the cause. Drunken devils are cast out
by ones, by sevens, and by legions. And
their unfortunate victims, like the poor
possessed, who was redeemed from his long
and lonely wanderings in the tombs, are
publishing to the ends of the earth, how
great things have been done for them.

To those new *champions* and this *new system* of tactics, our late success is mainly owing; and to them we must chiefly look for the final consummation. The ball is now rolling gloriously on, and none are so able as *they* to increase its speed and its bulk—to add to its momentum, and its magnitude. —Even though unlearned in letters, for this task, none others are so well educated. To fit them for this work, they have been taught in the true school. *They* have been in *that* gulf, from which they would teach others the means of escape. *They* have passed that prison wall, which others have long declared impassable; and who that has not, shall dare to weigh opinions with *them,* as to the mode of passing.

But if it be true, as I have insisted, that those who have suffered by intemperance, *personally,* and have reformed, are the most powerful and efficient instruments to push the reformation to ultimate success, it does not follow, that those who have not suffered, have no part left them to perform. Whether

or not the world would be vastly benefited
by a total and final banishment from it of
all intoxicating drinks, seems to me not *now*
to be an open question. Three-fourths of
mankind confess the affirmative with their
tongues, and, I believe, all the rest acknowledge it in their *hearts*.

Ought *any*, then, to refuse their aid in
doing what the good of the *whole* demands?
—Shall he, who cannot do *much*, be, for that
reason, excused if he do *nothing?* "But,"
says one, "what good can I do by signing
the pledge? I never drink even without
signing." This question has already been
asked and answered more than a million
times. Let it be answered once more. For
the man to suddenly, or in any other way,
to break off from the use of drams, who has
indulged in them for a long course of years,
and until his appetite for them has become
ten or a hundred-fold stronger, and more
craving, than any natural appetite can be,
requires a most powerful moral effort. In
such an undertaking, he needs every moral

support and influence, that can possibly be brought to his aid, and thrown around him. And not only so; but every moral prop should be taken *from* whatever argument might rise in his mind to lure him to his back-sliding. When he casts his eyes around him, he should be able to see all that he respects, all that he admires, and all that he loves, kindly and anxiously pointing him onward; and none beckoning him back, to his former miserable "wallowing in the mire."

But it is said by some, that men will *think* and *act* for themselves; that none will disuse spirits or anything else, merely because his neighbors do; and that *moral influence* is not that powerful engine contended for. Let us examine this. Let me ask the man who would maintain this position most stiffly, what compensation he will accept to go to church some Sunday and sit during the sermon with his wife's bonnet on his head? Not a trifle, I'll venture. And why not? There would be nothing irreligious in it; nothing immoral, nothing uncomfortable.—Then why not? Is it not because there would be something egregiously unfashionable in it? Then it is the influence of *fashion;* and what is the influence of fashion, but the influence that other people's actions have upon *our own* actions; the strong inclination each of us feels to do as we see all our neghbors do? Nor is the influence of fashion confined to any particular thing or class of things. It is just as strong on one subject as another. Let us make it as unfashionable to withhold our names from the temperance pledge as for husbands to wear their wives' bonnets to church, and instances will be just as rare in the one case as in the other.

"But," say some, "we are no drunkards; and we shall not acknowledge ourselves such by joining a reformed drunkards' society, whatever our influence might be." Surely no Christian will adhere to this objection.—If they believe, as they profess, that Omnipotence condescended to take on

himself the form of sinful man, as such, to
die an ignominous death for their sakes,
surely they will not refuse submission to the
infinitely lesser condescension, for the temporal, and perhaps eternal salvation, of a
large, erring, and unfortunate class of their
own fellow creatures. Nor is the condescension very great.

In my judgment, such of us as have never
fallen victims, have been spared more from
the absence of appetite, than from any men-
tal or moral superiority over those who
have. Indeed, I believe, if we take habitual
drunkards as a class, their heads and hearts
will bear an advantageous comparison with
those of any other class. There seems ever
to have been a proneness in the brilliant,
and the warm-blooded, to fall into this vice.
—The demon of intemperance ever seems to
have delighted in sucking the blood of
genius and of generosity. What one of us
but can call to mind some dear relative,
more promising in youth than all of his
fellows, who has fallen a sacrifice to his

rapacity? He ever seems to have gone
forth, like the Egyptian angel of death, com-
missioned to slay if not the first, the fairest
born of every family. Shall he now be
arrested in his desolating career? In that
arrest, all can give aid that will; and who
shall be excused that *can* and will not?
Far around as human breath has ever
blown, he keeps our fathers, our brothers,
our sons, and our friends, prostrate in the
chains of moral death. To all the living
everywhere, we cry, "Come, sound the moral
resurrection trump, that these may rise
and stand up, an exceeding great army"—
"Come from the four winds, O breath! and
breathe upon these slain, that they may
live."

If the relative grandeur of revolutions
shall be estimated by the great amount of
human misery they alleviate, and the small
amount they inflict, then, indeed, will this
be the grandest the world shall ever have
seen.—Of our political revolution of '76, we
all are justly proud. It has given us a de-

gree of political freedom, far exceeding that of any other of the nations of the earth. In it the world has found a solution of that long-mooted problem, as to the capability of man to govern himself. In it was the germ which has vegetated, and still is to grow and expand, into the universal liberty of mankind.

But with all these glorious results, past, present, and to come, it had its evils too.—It breathed forth famine, swam in blood and rode on fire; and long, long after, the orphan's cry, and widow's wail, continue to break the sad silence that ensued. These were the price, the inevitable price, paid for the blessings it bought.

Turn now, to the temperance revolution. In *it*, we shall find a stronger bondage broken; a viler slavery manumitted; a greater tyrant deposed. In *it*, more of want supplied, more disease healed, more sorrow assuaged. By *it*, no orphans starving, no widows weeping. By *it*, none wounded in feeling, none injured in interest. Even the dram maker, and the dram seller, will have glided into other occupations so *gradually,* as never to have felt the shock of change; and will stand ready to join all others in the universal song of gladness.

And what a noble ally this, to the cause of political freedom. With such an aid, its march cannot fail to be on and on, until every son on earth shall drink in rich fruition the sorrow-quenching draughts of perfect liberty. Happy day, when all appetites controlled, all passions subdued, all manners subjected, *mind,* all-conquering *mind,* shall live and move the monarch of the world. Glorious consummation! Hail, fall of Fury! Reign of Reason, all hail!

And when the victory shall be complete— when there shall be neither a slave nor a drunkard on earth—how proud the title of that *Land,* which may truly claim to be the birthplace and the cradle of both those revolutions, that shall have ended in that victory. How nobly distinguished that people, who shall have planted, and nurtured to maturity, both the political and moral freedom of their species.

This is the one hundred and tenth anniversary of the birthday of Washington.— We are met to celebrate this day. Washington is the mightiest name of earth—*long since* mightiest in the cause of civil liberty; *still* mightiest in moral reformation. On that name, a eulogy is expected. It cannot be. To add brightness to the sun, or glory to the name of Washington, is alike impossible. Let none attempt it. In solemn awe pronounce the name, and in its naked deathless splendor, leave it shining on.

If we take into consideration the day in which it was spoken, this is one of the most remarkable addresses ever delivered. It may be doubted if there was ever a grander temperance address delivered in the history of the world. It is remarkable for its breadth of vision and its sanity.

It is worth while to note the remark that

the cause in Lincoln's day had been harmed by the harsh methods and overbearing and unkind words of some speakers. The same is true to-day. It is as true now as in Lincoln's time that not abuse and hard names, but kindness and sympathy are essential if we would win men and women to our standard. The new movement—the Lincoln Legion—is pledged to the Lincoln spirit. Its work will be begun and fostered in harmony with the sentiment of him whose immortal name it bears upon its banner, " with malice toward none, with charity for all." Its motto enjoins three of the Great Master's qualities, which were found in a marked degree in Abraham Lincoln, " Love, Sacrifice, Service! "

FATHER MATTHEW AND HIS CAREER

There is no gratification worthy of a Christian that cannot be enjoyed without tasting intoxicating liquors.

The pledge which I ask you and others to take does not enslave, it makes free—free from vice, free from passion, free from an enslaving habit.—FATHER MATTHEW.

CHAPTER IV

FATHER MATTHEW AND HIS CAREER

FATHER MATTHEW had been for some years one of the Governors of the House of Industry, the Cork Workhouse of those days—in which the poor waifs and strays of society, the wretched and the broken-down, the victims of their own folly, or of the calamities, accidents, and vicissitudes of life, found a miserable home. Father Matthew was a big-hearted, sincerely Christian man, and he saw so much of the ruin wrought by strong drink that it made of him a total abstainer.

On the Board of Governors, with Father Matthew, was one who, himself a convert to the doctrine of total abstinence, never failed to direct his attention to any case more remarkable in its distressing features than another, with the observation—" Strong drink is the cause of this." And having excited the compassionate sympathy of his associate, he would add, " Oh, Theobald Matthew! If thou would only give thy aid, much good could be done in this city."

This friend, William Martin, by name, was a persistent soul, and did not easily give up when once he had put his hand to the plow. He had made up his mind that Father Matthew, who was the most popular and influential priest in that portion of Ireland, was the man above all others to lead in a great movement against the habit of strong drink, and so, again and again, he rang the words in his friend's ears, " Oh, Theobald Matthew, if thou would but take the cause in hand." Father Matthew was now in his forty-seventh year, and had had large experience both among the rich and among the poor. In every class of society he had witnessed the devastation wrought by this monster iniquity. Although for a long time he gave no sign, Martin's cease-less reiteration at last made itself felt, and seemed to be to him the call of God. On a day early in April, 1838, William Martin received a message from Father Matthew asking him to call on him that evening. Father Matthew met him at the door, saying, "Welcome, Mr. Martin, welcome, my dear friend. It is very kind of you to come to me at so short a notice, and so punctually, too."

"I was right glad to come to thee, Theobald Matthew, for I expected that thou had good news for me."

"Well, Mr. Martin, I have sent for you to assist me in forming a temperance society in this neighborhood."

"I knew it!" exclaimed Martin; "something seemed to tell me that thou would'st do it at last."

The meeting was called, and not a very large crowd came together. Father Matthew took the chair, and made an address, in the course of which he said:

"These gentlemen are good enough to say that I could be useful in promoting the great

virtue of temperance, and arresting the
spread of drunkenness. I am quite alive to
the evils which this vice brings with it,
especially to the humbler classes, who are
naturally most exposed to its temptation,
and liable to yield to its seductive influences.
I have always endeavored, as a minister of
religion, to discourage drunkenness, not
with the success I desired, it is true; but I
yielded to no one in my wish to see our working classes sober and self-respecting. I
could not refuse to listen to the many appeals
made to me. Your respected friend, Mr.
Martin, has often asked me to do what I am
about to do this night. . . My dear friends,
I much fear that your kind partiality has
made you overlook my many defects, and
attribute to me merits which I am very far
from possessing; but if, through any humble
instrumentality of mine, I can do good to
my fellow creatures, and give glory to God,
I feel I am bound, as a minister of the Gospel, to throw all personal considerations
aside, and try and give a helping hand to

gentlemen who have afforded me so excellent
an example. Indeed, if only one poor soul
could be rescued from destruction by what
we are now attempting, it would be giving
glory to God, and well worth all the trouble
we could take. No person in health has
any need of intoxicating drinks. My dear
friends, you don't require them, nor do I
require them—neither do I take them.
Many of you here have proved that they can
be done without, for you are strong in health
and in the possession of your faculties.
After much reflection on the subject, I have
come to the conviction that there is no neces-
sity for them, for anyone in good health;
and I advise you all to follow my example.
I will be the first to sign my name in the
book which is on the table, and I hope we
shall soon have it full."

Father Matthew then approached the
table, and, taking the pen, said, in a voice
heard by all, and remembered by those present for many years—"Here goes, in the
name of God!" and signed his name in

full.   Some sixty others followed him that evening.

The work was successful from the first. The Society was formed in April, 1838, and by January, 1839, over two hundred thousand members had signed its roll in Cork and the adjoining counties.

In December, 1839, Father Matthew made his first missionary visitation as the apostle of total abstinence.   This visit was made to the city of Limerick, and wrought that ancient city to great excitement.   The people came in from the country round about and packed the streets.   Father Matthew's reception was an ovation such as few men ever received; indeed still fewer had ever excited in the people the same blended feelings of love, and reverence, and enthusiasm. For four days Father Matthew preached and exhorted so long as the least remnant of a voice was left him.   His mission was marvelously successful.   In those four days one hundred and fifty thousand men and women signed the total abstinence pledge,

Almarinda Bell Galloway.　　R. E. Berry.　　Moses Martin.　　Cleopas Breckenridge.

SURVIVORS OF THE LINCOLN MEETING AT SOUTH FORK SCHOOLHOUSE, 1847.

A reunion of the pledge-signers, June, 1903.

and joined the growing total-abstinence
ranks.

Many amusing things occurred illustrat-
ing the humor and peculiar characteristics
of the Irish temperament. During his mission in Waterford, as Father Matthew was
about to mark the sign of the cross on the
forehead of a native who showed every indication of close acquaintance with the
drink, the man clutched Father Matthew by
the skirts of his coat with such a grasp as a
drunken man can take, and, in a voice much
broken by hiccoughs, cried out,—" Father
Matthew, darlin', you m-m-ust k-k-iss
me!" " My dear, do let me go. God bless
you, my dear child; be a good boy for the
future. There—do let me go," said Father
Matthew. " No, Father Matthew, darlin',
I won't l-l-ave go my hoult till I get wan
k-k-iss!" " Oh, my dear, do let me go!"
" No; wan is all I ax, an' I m-m-ust have it.
Don't r-r-efuse a poor fellow craychure wan
kiss—only wan!" persisted the tender soul.
A number of gentlemen and clergymen tried

to induce the man to quit his hold on Father Matthew's coat; but all in vain. Jim was determined to have his " wan kiss." " Jim, avick, aren't you ashamed of yourself—the holy priest!—an' in the chapel, too!" remonstrated an old woman near him. " Jim, you bosthoon, you! Quit yer hould of his reverence this moment!" insisted a sturdy friend at the other side. " No, not till I get wan k-k-iss; no, af I died for it, I won't lave go."

Father Matthew, seeing that unpleasant consequences were likely to ensue if Jim's rather inconvenient request was not at once complied with, resolved to make him happy, and accordingly kissed Jim on both cheeks, saying, " Now, James, my dear, go home and remain quiet, and be a sensible boy for the future." The " boy " was not much short of forty years of age. Jim relinquished his grasp of the skirt of the coat, and retired proud of his achievement.

The fame of Father Matthew rapidly spread abroad throughout the island. It may be doubted if there has ever been such enthusiasm manifested in any reform movement as was shown by the followers of Father Matthew. Father Matthew was once on his way by coach from Dublin to Cork. The coach stopped at the town of Athy, long enough to permit the passengers to have breakfast at the hotel. One of the group waiting before the hotel recognized Father Matthew, and shouted the news in the street, "Father Matthew is at the hotel!" The people began to gather, and by the time breakfast was over, thousands were wedged about the coach, so that it could not start. They demanded to receive the pledge from his hand. He had them kneel down in great long rows, and pledged them one after another. But as fast as he got rid of one large batch, another much larger took its place—and all this time the crowd becoming more dense, in consequence of frequent accessions from the surrounding country; so that it was not until after a delay of five hours, during which Father Matthew worked as he never worked before in his life, that the Royal Mail Coach was well out of the town of Athy.

In 1844 Father Matthew paid a visit to England, where he was received with the greatest kindness and enthusiasm on all sides, and in the course of a campaign of a few weeks six hundred thousand persons took the pledge of total abstinence, and even this could not estimate the good which he did, for an eye-witness writing of it at the time said: "It is a matter of little difficulty to compute the numbers who knelt before Father Matthew and received the pledge at his hands; but it would be a difficult task, indeed, to tell the good which he accomplished, the fallen whom he raised, the erring whom he brought back to virtue, the despairing whom he comforted, the hungry and the naked whom he fed and clad."

Dr. Theodore L. Cuyler has given a most interesting account in his "Recollections of a Long Life," of meeting Father Matthew in Scotland, and of making his first youthful temperance address in his presence. Dr. Cuyler says:

" When I made my first visit to Edinburgh in 1842, I learned that a temperance society of that city was about to go over to Glasgow to meet the celebrated Father Theobald Matthew, who was making his first visit to Scotland. I joined my Edinburgh friends, and on arriving in Glasgow we found a multitude of over fifty thousand people assembled on the green. In an open barouche, drawn by four horses, stood a short, stout Irishman, with a handsome benevolent countenance, and attired in a long black coat, with a silver medal hanging upon his breast. After the procession, headed by his carriage, had forced its way through the densely thronged street, it halted in a small open square. Father Matthew dismounted, and began to administer the pledge of abstinence to those who were willing to receive it. They kneeled on the ground in platoons; the pledge was read aloud to them; Father Matthew laid his hands upon them, and pronounced a benediction. From the necks of many a small medal attached to a cord was suspended. In this rapid manner, the pledge was administered to many hundreds of persons within an hour, and fresh crowds continually came forward.

" When I was introduced to the good man as an American, he spoke a few kind words, and gave me an " apostolic kiss " upon my cheek. As I was about to make the first public speech of my life, I suppose that I may regard that act of the great Irish apostle as a sort of ordination to the ministry of preaching the Gospel of Total Abstinence. The administration of the pledge was followed by a grand meeting of welcome in the City Hall. Father Matthew spoke with modest simplicity and deep emotion, attributing all his wonderful success to the direct blessings of God upon his efforts to persuade his fellow-men to throw off the despotism of the bottle. After delivering my maiden speech, I hastened back to Edinburgh with the deputation from 'Auld Reekie,' and I never saw Father Matthew again. He was, unquestionably, the most remarkable temperance reformer who has yet appeared."

In 1849, Father Matthew paid a long-contemplated visit to America, and on the second day of July of that year the City of New York bade him a most remarkable welcome. The Municipal Council, accompanied by deputations from various public bodies and societies, met him at Staten Island on a steamer to conduct him to Castle Garden, where his arrival was awaited by an immense assembly. The ships in the harbor were covered with flags, strains of music floated in the air, and cheers were heard from many a vessel as the steamer bearing Father Matthew proceeded up the harbor. Of course, the wild ringing cheers of the Irish could be heard above all, as they occupied every vantage ground that enabled them to catch a glimpse of their beloved countryman, from whose hands many thousands among them had received the pledge in the old country.

Mayor Woodhull, in his speech of welcome to Father Matthew, said:

" On this spot we have been accustomed to receive the most distinguished men of our own and other lands. The statesman, bearing the highest honors of his much loved country, and the victor, fresh from the field of his proud triumphs, have here been greeted with the salutations of the most elevated in authority, and with the general welcome of the citizens of this metropolis. But you, sir, come among us with a highly different and peculiar distinction. The honors which you wear have been accorded to you by those who revere you for your deeds of love and benevolence. Your titles are written on the hearts of the uncounted masses whom your heroic perseverance in the humble acts of mercy and good will have saved from a fate even more dreadful than the grave. Your victories are not made up of the dead and dying left behind in your path, but of living thousands whom you have rescued from a fate more remorseless than the conqueror's march. Your trophies are seen in the smiling faces and happy homes of the countless multitudes whom you have won from the deepest abyss of wretchedness and despair. The enemy with whom you have grappled is one of the direst to the human race. Frightful are the ravages of plague, and vast the preparations to stay its desolating curse; but the destroying angel of Intemperance has entombed more victims than any pestilence which has ever afflicted the human family. All seasons are its own, and no physician can baffle its downward progress. Quarantines and sanitary precautions cannot check its career. Yet there is one human power that can subdue the enemy of man. It is the moral power of a persuasive, earnest, and benevolent heart, that summons all its affections, and with heroic subblimity, concentrates all its energies to the single work to be accomplished. It is this power which you have so successfully exercised, and by which you have attained such astonishing results."

In the evening of the day of the reception, the Common Council of New York City entertained Father Matthew at a public dinner, at which all healths were drunk, and all toasts honored, in glasses of pure "Croton." "There is as much sincerity," said the great temperance reformer, "in water as in wine; and I beg to give, in a full bumper of this pure liquid, the health and prosperity of the Mayor and citizens of New York."

For the two weeks following his wonderful welcome to New York City, Father Matthew held levees in City Hall, which was daily thronged with visitors of every class and condition, and representing every sect and nationality in the United States. So great was the inconvenience from crowding on the first two days that it became necessary to have one day set apart for the reception of ladies, and the next for the reception of gentlemen.

Father Matthew's visit to America gave an immense impulse to the temperance movement, which was felt not only where he spoke, and by those who came under the magic of his presence, but by multitudes in far-distant sections of the country who were never permitted to look upon his face. It is, of course, impossible to tell how much influence the movement led by Father Matthew had on the mind of Abraham Lincoln, and his decision, both by example and precept, to stand for total abstinence. It is an interesting fact, however, to note that the same Sangamon *Weekly Journal,* a paper which Lincoln constantly read, and which published Lincoln's temperance address, given in a previous chapter, contained at length, frequent references to Father Matthew's work, and quotations from his addresses.

THE WASHINGTONIANS AND OTHER
TOTAL ABSTINENCE SOCIETIES

When I compare the past with the present, my days of intemperance with my present peace and sobriety, my past degradation with my present position in this hall—the Cradle of Liberty—I am overwhelmed. It seems to me holy ground.

*I never expected to see this hall. I heard of it in my boyhood. 'Twas here that Otis and the elder Adams argued the principles of independence, and we now meet here to make a second declaration of independence, not quite so lengthy as the old one, but it promises life, liberty, and the pursuit of happiness. Our forefathers pledged their lives, their fortunes, and their sacred honor; we, too, will pledge our honor and our lives, but our fortunes—they have gone for rum!—*JOHN HAWKINS, *the Leader of the Washingtonians, in a speech at Faneuil Hall, Boston.*

CHAPTER V

THE WASHINGTONIANS AND OTHER TOTAL ABSTINENCE SOCIETIES

PERHAPS no reform movement in the world ever had so unique a beginning as the Washingtonian movement. It had its origin in the city of Baltimore, in the year 1840, in a liquor saloon. Half a dozen men who were hard topers had organized themselves into a club, and they used to meet and have their sprees in Chase's Tavern. One night a distinguished temperance lecturer, the Rev. Matthew Hale Smith, was billed to speak in one of the churches, and this drunkards' club, in some freak spirit, appointed two of their number a committee to go and hear him. The committee were very much impressed with the arguments and appeals which they heard, and when they came back with a favorable report, there was a very heated discussion in the club. The saloon-keeper overheard their talk, and at once burst forth in a tirade of abuse against all temperance lecturers, denouncing them as fools and hypocrites.

In reply to the saloon-keeper, one man was sober enough to respond, " Of course it is for your interest to cry them down "; whereupon the discussion waxed hotter and hotter, and the marvelous result of the debate was that the six men formed themselves into a temperance club, which they styled the " Washingtonian Total Abstinence Society," and adopted a pledge requiring total abstinence from the use of all intoxicating drinks.

The names of these six individuals were William K. Mitchell, John F. Hoss, David Anderson, George Stears, James McCurley, and Archibald Campbell. John Hawkins early became a member, and was the most important figure during the early and growing development of the movement, but was not one of the original six. They voted to meet the next night in a carpenter shop, and each agreed to bring a new member. For a long time they met nearly every night, and, naturally, before a great while, their meetings attracted public attention.

These reformed men soon received invitations to other cities and towns; the movement spread from city to city, and from town to town, until there was scarcely a thickly inhabited community in the United States that did not have its Washingtonian Total Abstinence Society. Men who had been drunkards for years burst the bonds that had so long bound them, and became temperance reformers. Indeed, the entire movement was unique in that it had begun among the drinkers themselves, and as such it immediately became famous. It was largely carried on through many men telling their own experience, and many drunkards that could not have been reached by the oratory of the most eloquent speaker, were reached through the stumbling story of another man who had himself been in the toils of strong drink and knew its temptations and its sorrows.

The most striking figure in the early days of the Washingtonian movement was John Hawkins. He was born in Baltimore, on the 28th of September, 1797. After some years at the school of the Rev. Mr. Coxe, at the age of fourteen he was apprenticed for eight years to learn the trade of a hatter with a master whose place of business was a regular den of drunkenness. Of the sixty men who were working there at the time he entered, every man died a drunkard.

When the British made a landing at Baltimore during the War of 1812, young Hawkins borrowed a musket and joined the ranks of the volunteers, exposing himself with all the rashness and abandon of Southern youth, in the very front of the battle, from which, however, he escaped unhurt. Afterwards he went West, where he became not only a drunkard, but a vagabond. He says of himself:

"For six months I had no shoes, and

only one shirt and one pair of pantaloons. Then I was a vagabond, indeed, but I returned, ragged and bloated, to my mother's home.

"When I got to the edge of my native town I was so ashamed that I waited till the dusk of the evening, and then I crept along to the house of my mother. She dressed me up decently, did not upbraid me, but only said, ' John, I am afraid you are bloated!'"

Young Hawkins, having temporarily reformed, was married on Christmas Day, 1822, to Miss Rachel Thompson, of Baltimore, of which marriage two children were born, Elizabeth and Hannah. He did better for a good while, but then grew worse until he became a confirmed sot. He writes of his condition:

"During the first two weeks of June, 1840, I drank dreadfully, bought liquor by the gallon, and drank and drank. I cannot tell how I suffered; in body everything, but in mind more!

"By the 14th of the month—drunk all

the time—I was a wonder to myself, astonished that I had any mind left; and yet it seemed, in the goodness of God, uncommonly clear. My conscience drove me to madness. I hated the darkness of the night, and when morning came, I hated the light; I hated myself, hated existence; was about taking my own life. I asked myself, ' Can I restrain? Is it possible? ' But there was no one to take me by the hand, and say *you can*. I had a pint of whisky in my room, where I lay in bed, and thought I would drink it, but this seemed to be a turning point with me. I know it was life or death, as I decided to drink it or not.

" My wife came up, knowing how I was suffering, and asked me to come down to breakfast. I said I would come presently. Then my daughter Hannah came up—my only friend, I always loved her the most—and she said:

" ' Father, don't send me after whisky to-day! '

" I was tormented before; this was agony.

I could not stand it, so I told her to leave, and she went downstairs crying, and saying, ' Father is angry with me.' My wife came up again, and asked me to take some coffee. I told her I did not want anything of her, and covered myself up in bed. Pretty soon I heard someone in the room, and, peeping out, I saw it was my daughter.

" ' Hannah,' said I, ' I'm not angry with you—and—I shall not drink any more.' Then we wept together.

" I got up, went to the cupboard and looked on my enemy, the whisky bottle, and thought, ' Is it possible I can be restored? ' Several times while dressing I looked at the bottle, but I thought, ' I shall be lost if I yield.'

" Well, I went to the society of reformed drunkards, where I found all my old bottle companions. I did not tell anyone, not even my wife, that I was going. I had got out of difficulty, but did not know how long I could keep out.

" The six founders of the Society were

there.   We had worked together, got drunk together, we stuck together like brothers.

" One of them said, ' Here's Hawkins, the regulator, the old bruiser,' and they clapped and laughed, but there was no laugh in me, I was too solemn and sober for that.   Then they read the pledge:

" 'We, whose names are annexed, desirous of forming a Society for our mutual benefit and to guard against a pernicious practice which is injurious to our health, standing, and families, do pledge ourselves as gentlemen, that we will not drink any spirituous or malt liquors, wine, or cider.'

" They all looked over my shoulder to see me write my name.   It was a great battle. I never had such feelings before.

" At eleven o'clock I went home.   Before when I stayed out late I always went home drunk.   My yard was covered with brick, and my wife could easily tell as I walked over it whether I was drunk or sober.   She could even tell whether the gate opened drunk or sober.

"Well, this time it opened sober, and when I entered she was astonished. I smiled, and she smiled; and then I told her quick—I could not keep it back:

"*'I have put my name to the temperance pledge, never to drink as long as I live.'*

"It was a happy time. I cried and she cried—we couldn't help it—the crying woke up my daughter, and she cried too for joy. I slept none that night; my thoughts were better than sleep. Next morning I went to see my mother. She had been praying twenty years for her drunken son. When she heard the good news she said, 'It is enough. Now I am ready to die.'"

The Washingtonian meetings might have been called temperance class meetings. Reformed men went about telling their experience, and that encouraged others. In one of his meetings in Faneuil Hall, Boston, John Hawkins said:

"Drunkard! come up here! You can reform. I met a gentleman this morning who reformed four weeks ago, rejoicing in his reformation; he brought a man with him who took the pledge, and this man brought two others. This is the way we do the business up in Baltimore. We reformed drunkards are a Committee of the Whole on the State of the Union. We are all missionaries. We don't slight the drunkard; we love him, we nurse him, as a mother does her infant learning to walk."

During its days of popularity the Washingtonian meetings were often enthusiastic and excited to the last degree; the experiences of men who had been notorious for their drunkenness and debauchery now actually reformed, presented an argument that nothing could resist, and when they appeared on a platform at a meeting, it seemed like a miracle to the people. In the back part of the audience poor drunken creatures would rise up, and, with a look of desperation on their whisky-bloated faces, would cry out:

"Do you think I could reform? Do you think there is any hope for me?"

"Yes, brother. Sign the pledge, and it will make a sober man of you," would be the reply. Then, amid the sobs and "God bless you's" of his family and friends, as well as scores of those who had but lately escaped from the enemy, the poor drunkard would find his way trembling to the platform and write his name, while the whole audience seemed to hold its breath, and tears were on every face.

That the Washingtonian movement did great good is beyond all cavil. The good done by it was so great that the temperance question has been on a higher level ever since. For a time it produced a revolution in the drinking habits of the country. The weak spot in the Washingtonian movement seems to have been in the fact that many of the leaders of the movement, instead of feeling the need of religion to strengthen and sustain the human will, declared that religious exercises were out of place in temperance meetings, and would not consent for the meeting to be opened with prayer. By leaders of this type the movement as divorced from the churches, to its infinite loss. Of course, this was not always the case, and oftentimes where pastors were wise, great revivals of religion followed a Washingtonian campaign, and Christian ministers as a rule were naturally earnest supporters of the movement.

The Washingtonian movement was thought by some of the earnest leaders of the day to lack the element of permanency. In every city thousands of people united with the Society and took the total abstinence pledge who had been victims of strong drink. Indeed, John Hawkins declared that under the influence of the Washingtonian meetings four-fifths of all the drunkards in Boston had signed the temperance pledge. It was felt that these men who had been so under the power of the drinking habit, needed more care and fraternal fellowship than could be given by so informal a society as the Washingtonians. With this thought in mind, there sprang up after a few

PRESTON BRECKENRIDGE,

The father of Cleopas Breckenridge, who induced
Lincoln to hold the meeting at South Fork
Schoolhouse, 1847.

CLEOPAS BRECKENRIDGE,

Who signed the pledge when 10 years old at the
Lincoln meeting at South Fork Schoolhouse,
1847.

years many fraternal organizations having for their base-work of purpose the total abstinence pledge.

One of the first, and perhaps the most important in its time, was known as the Sons of Temperance. Abraham Lincoln was a member of this organization. It had its birth in New York City in 1842, at Teetotaler's Hall, which stood at 71 Division Street. This Society gave four dollars a week to members during sickness and in case of death thirty dollars was appropriated for funeral expenses. The pledge was as follows:

" I will neither make, buy, sell, nor use as a beverage, any spirituous or malt liquors, wine, or cider." This Society had a tremendous vogue. Its pledge was administered to three millions of men and women, and its influence for good covered the whole land.

Next in importance, perhaps, in widespread influence, is the Independent Order of Good Templars. Its platform is as follows:

First: Total abstinence from all intoxicating liquors as a beverage.

Second: No license, in any form or under any circumstances, for the sale of such liquors to be used as a beverage.

Third: Absolute prohibition of the manufacture, importation, and sale of intoxicating liquors for such purposes—prohibition by the will of the people, expressed in due form of law, with the penalties deserved for a crime of such enormity.

Fourth: The creation of a healthy public opinion upon the subject by the dissemination of the truth.

Fifth: The election of good and honest men to administer the laws.

Sixth: Persistence in efforts toward ultimate and universal success.

In the Sons of Temperance, the pledge is only binding during a membership in the order. But the Good Templar total abstinence pledge is for life. It is estimated that during the history of the order more than three millions of people have been initiated, and at one time nearly seven hundred thousand names were upon its rolls. Space does not permit me to tell the story of " The Temple of Honor," " The Independent Order of Rechabites," " The Independent Order of Good Samaritans and Daughters of Samaria," "The Friends of Temperance," " The United Friends of Temperance," " The Cadets of Temperance," " The Band of Hope," and many others.

The National Temperance Society and Publication House was organized in 1865, for the special work of creating and circulating a sound temperance literature to promote the cause of total abstinence from all intoxicants, and to unify and concentrate the Temperance and Christian sentiments against the drink habit and the drink traffic. The Society is genuinely non-partisan, and non-sectarian, and on its Board of Managers are representatives of all the great leading religious denominations and temperance organizations of the country. The Hon. William E. Dodge, the Rev. Dr. Mark Hopkins, the Rev. Dr. Theodore L. Cuyler, General O. O. Howard, Mr. Joshua L. Baily, and the Rev. Dr. D. Stuart Dodge, the present president, have in turn stood at the head of this useful organization. During the years since its foundation it has issued over twenty-two hundred different publications, printed and circulated two billion pages of temperance literature, and in this, and other missionary work, has disbursed over one and a half millions of dollars.

The Society publishes *The National Temperance Advocate,* a sixteen-page monthly for adults, *The Youth's Temperance Banner,* a four-page illustrated paper for children, and *The Water Lily,* designed for the kindergarten age. Many of the most earnest and faithful temperance workers of the past and present generation have wrought heroically, and often with great personal sacrifice, through this Society. Among the names of its most faithful workers is that of the late Mr. James N. Stearns, a life-long warrior for temperance, and the present editor of the Society's publications, the Rev. Dr. James B. Dunn.

It is interesting as an illustration of a fact often commented upon, that at the birth of any great movement for reform, as at the perfection of any great invention, it is always found that men in different parts of the world are thinking about the same things, and working toward the same ends. It is certainly an encouraging indication that the times are ripe for a new and world-wide movement for total abstinence through the temperance pledge method, that the National Temperance Society in the autumn of 1902, sought to inaugurate a revival of total abstinence preaching, securing by correspondence and personal appeal sermons in thousands of churches, and special services in Sabbath schools where the temperance pledge was circulated. Already the Society has sent out two and a half millions of pledges.

The Catholic Total Abstinence Union of America, the first Catholic Convention on

this continent for the promotion of total
abstinence, was held in the city of Baltimore
in the year 1872.

When Father Matthew was in this country in 1849, he organized a number of societies which kept up their existence, and
which served to form a link between the old
and the new epoch in Catholic total abstinence work; but in 1860 only about twelve
of these societies were in existence.

In 1860 a young priest, the Rev. Patrick
Byrne, became an assistant to one of the
pastors in Jersey City.   He asked permission of his superior to attempt the es-
tablishment of a religious total abstinence
society, which was given, and the Parochial
Total Abstinence Society was founded.
The founder says of it himself:

" I felt from the first the frightful nature
of this vice, and I determined to combat it
to the last limit allowed me by the Church;
but I soon found that an occasional sermon,
however powerful and scathing, or the administration of the pledge now and then,

either within or without the tribunal of
penance, was of little avail against a vice
which had interlaced itself with all the
social customs of our people. I therefore
began to establish society against society."

These societies have spread throughout
the union, and many distinguished Catholic
clergymen, notably Archbishop Ireland,
have given great and powerful support to
the temperance movement. There is perhaps nothing more hopeful for the future of
the temperance cause in America, than the
utterances already made and the promise
of advancement to more pronounced attitude in favor of total abstinence, and the
destruction of the saloon, by the Catholic
Church.

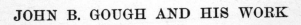

JOHN B. GOUGH AND HIS WORK

Let us reverently ask God to bless us for his great name's sake, and we with those we have worked for shall stand saved, not by our own efforts alone but by our own efforts blessed and acknowledged by Him in whose hands are the destinies of all men.—JOHN B. GOUGH.

CHAPTER VI

JOHN B. GOUGH AND HIS WORK

ON the last Sunday afternoon in October, 1842, a drunkard stumbled out from a humble house in the city of Worcester, Massachusetts. He was about half drunk at the time, and the flush of the liquor was on his face. He had a great sense of disgust and hatred for the drink, and yet was so under the power of it that he started to go down the street to the nearest saloon to get more liquor.

Just then he felt a kind touch on the shoulder. He turned his head to look into the eyes of a stranger.

" Mr. Gough, I believe," said the man who had touched him.

" Yes," was the answer, " but you have the advantage of me."

" My name is Stratton—Joel Stratton.

I'm a waiter yonder, in the Temperance Hotel. You've been drinking to-day."

Stratton's manner was so considerate and friendly that Gough could not take offense.

" Yes," he said, " I have."

" Why don't you sign the pledge? "

" I have no will, no hope, no future— nothing. The drink has eaten out my soul. Alcohol, which preserves snakes, destroys men. I couldn't keep the pledge if I took it. My dreadful condition is that I at once hate rum and crave it."

Stratton put his arm through that of the young man, and walked slowly on with him.

" You were once respectable," he said; " wouldn't you like to be so again? To have friends, to be a useful member of society? "

" I should like it first rate," retorted Gough; " but I have no expectation that such a thing will ever happen."

" Only sign our pledge," urged Stratton, " and I will warrant that it shall be so. Sign it, and I will myself introduce you to good friends who will feel an interest in your welfare and take pleasure in helping you to keep your good resolutions. Only sign the pledge, Mr. Gough, and all will be as I have said; aye, and more, too."

So kind, so earnest, and so hopeful was Mr. Stratton that it aroused buried hopes and ambitions in the poor drunkard, and with some decision of voice he said:

" I will sign the pledge."

" When? " asked his new friend. Gough hesitated a moment, and then said: " I can't do it to-night. I must have some more drink presently, but I certainly will to-morrow."

" We have a temperance meeting in the town hall to-morrow evening," said Stratton. " Will you take the pledge then? "

" I will! "

" That is right," was the hearty response. " I will be there to see you."

" You shall," said Gough. And they parted. Sure enough, the next night Gough, trembling and despairing, was in the hall at the temperance meeting. He was ragged, and looked the disreputable being he felt himself to be. A call was made for the relation of experiences. Acting under sudden impulse, Gough rose and told his wretched story. That was his first temperance speech.

Joel Stratton was there on the lookout for him, and when Gough got through with his terrible story he brought him the pledge and gave him the pen, and Gough signed it in rambling, crooked characters.

The meeting was held once a week in the temperance hall, and the next Monday night, when the time for the experiences came around, Gough rose and said:

" I am getting on very well, and feel a good deal better than I did a week ago."

This was Gough's second temperance address. He was to be the most famous orator which the nineteenth century produced in the defense of sobriety and total abstinence, and indeed, his eloquence and oratorical power in after years amounted to no less than genius. But all these had been

wasted by the drink, and would never have
been dreamed of except for his reformation.
His ability to speak came to be manifest by
degrees. At the weekly temperance meetings he usually uttered a few sentences.
Gradually, he enlarged upon the theme, his
passion kindled, his humor gained freedom,
and his pathos self-respect. It was not long
before he was invited to repeat the story of
his experience in other towns within the
reach of Worcester. Thus he felt his way
into wider notice and usefulness as a
speaker. At this time nothing was farther
from his thoughts than that he would ever
make temperance lecturing a business.
This went on for a long time. His oratory
grew through months of practice in country
schoolhouses; countless verbal repetitions
of his biography, aided in the development
of his powers. He worked in a book-
binder's-shop all day, and then walked or
rode in the evening to his appointment in
some near-by town.

Gough's meetings were usually held in

schoolhouses, and often other speakers took part. At a gathering in West Boylston, Massachusetts, Gough first occupied the whole evening, and earned his first lecture-fee, which amounted to two dollars, so that the occasion was always memorable to him. Finally the local demands for his services so increased that he took off his apron, left the book-bindery, and began his career as a temperance orator.

For years John B. Gough had hard work and poor pay. Of the first year he says: " In 365 days I gave 383 addresses, and received for them $1059—out of which I paid my traveling expenses; traveled 6840 miles; and obtained 15,218 signatures to the pledge." He could have earned a great deal more money at bookbinding, but his heart was set now upon something better than making money. Sometimes, however, the meanness or lack of thought on the part of his audience, put him in trying circumstances. One year his average pay for a lecture was $2.77! He tells a story of one

case as follows: "Once, after I had been
speaking for nearly two hours, and had
taken my seat, the chairman rose, and proposed a vote of thanks, which was passed
unanimously. As the audience were being
dismissed, I asked if that vote of thanks
' could be given me in writing? as perhaps
the conductor on the train would take it for
my fare.' The hint was sufficient, and a
collection was taken up, amounting to four
dollars."

No sketch of John B. Gough is adequate
that does not refer to the noble fidelity of
Mary Whitcomb Gough, the young Yankee
school-ma'am, to whom the orator was
married November 24, 1843. Gough says of
her: " She took me on trust, with $3.50 in
my pocket; but Mary was willing to risk it
with me."

No wife was ever a greater blessing to a
husband than Mary Gough was to hers.
For a great many years she accompanied
him wherever he went. Her care prolonged
his life, and made it doubly useful.

Gough's manner of speaking was so exhausting to him, that when he closed a lecture he was dripping with perspiration; his clothes were often wringing wet; his vitality was spent; he was in a state of collapse. Hours of skillful attention were necessary in order to soothe him into quietude. He had to be recuperated with bath and food; nor did sleep come until long past midnight. His wife was his constant companion, and his skillful loving nurse. No wonder Gough's common phrase about her was, "My brave, faithful Mary!"

After their marriage Gough and his wife went to Boston; where the proud husband introduced his bride to his good friend and supporter, Deacon Grant. The good deacon was much interested in Gough, and had been afraid he would make a poor choice of a wife. He looked the young wife over most carefully for a few moments, and then said:

"John, she'll do!"

And Gough, recalling the incident a

quarter of a century later, said: " Nobly she has done."

No one can understand the career of John B. Gough who leaves out of consideration the great fact that it was a service rendered with most devout and unselfish desire to serve God and his fellow-men. On one occasion when the terms offered him for his work were such that they could barely live, he remarked to his wife that they were not likely to get rich on such terms. But Mary Gough bravely answered:

" No matter, John. We are doing the Lord's work."

It is interesting to note that though Gough's power as a speaker developed very slowly at first, that after he began to speak every day, it was not long before he became conspicious for true eloquence. In 1844 he spoke at a great temperance convention in Faneuil Hall, Boston. It was on this occasion that he is believed first to have introduced his apostrophe to water, which soon became famous across the continent.

Holding in his hand a glass filled with it, he said:

"Is not this beautiful? Talk of ruby wine. Here is our beverage—water, pure water; we drink it to quench our thirst. There is no occasion to drink except to quench one's thirst; and here is the beverage our Father has provided for his children. When Moses smote the rock the people were thirsty, and it was water that came forth, not wine, or rum, or ale. Were you ever thirsty, with lips dry and feverish, and throat parched? Did you ever lift the goblet of pure water to your lips and feel it trickling over the tongue and gurgling down the throat? Was it not luxury? Give to the traveler on the burning desert, as he lies perishing with thirst, a goblet of cold water, and he will return the goblet heaping with gold; give him wine, rum, or ale, and he turns away in feverish disgust to die. Our beverage is beautiful and pure, for God brewed it—not in the distillery, but out of the earth."

The late E. W. Metcalf,
of Elyria, Ohio.

Mr. A. I. Root,
of Medina, Ohio.

TWO OF THE EARLY SUPPORTERS OF THE ANTI-SALOON LEAGUE.

Little by little Gough's fame grew as a lecturer until it was no longer confined to America. He made several trips to Europe, and became as popular in England and Ireland and Scotland as in this country. He never forgot the pit from which he was dug, nor the power of kindness to reach a despairing heart, nor the benefit of signing a pledge to abstain from intoxicating drink.

Hundreds of thousands of men and women and children signed the pledge under the influence of his impassioned appeals. He did untold good. Here is a story which may stand as a typical one, fairly representing thousands of instances of a similar character.

On one occasion Mr. Gough was in Covent Garden, London, when a man came to him, and said:

" Mr. Gough, I want you to come into my place of business."

" I'm in a little hurry now," Gough replied.

"You *must* come into my place of business."

Mr. Gough yielded to his entreaties, and followed him into a large fruit store, where he was doing business to the amount of fifteen hundred dollars a week. As soon as they were safe in the store from the street, the man turned and caught Gough by the hand, and said:

"God bless you, sir!"

"What for?"

"I heard you in Exeter Hall a year and a half ago, and signed the pledge. I was a brute."

"No, you were not."

"Well, I was worse."

"No, you were not."

"Well, I was as bad as I could be. Look at that cellar! I spent a whole Sunday in that cellar on a heap of rotten vegetables, with a rope to hang myself by! Now, sir, I lease that cellar and clear a hundred pounds a year, God bless you, sir! See what a business I am doing. Look here! See that woman in the corner? She's my wife. La! How I have knocked her about. Would you go and shake hands with her?"

"I have no objection."

"Do, sir."

Gough went up to her, and offered his hand. She held back, and said, "My fingers are so sticky with the fruit, sir."

"La!" said the husband. "Mr. Gough don't mind sticky fingers."

Gough shook hands with her, heartily, and says, "Our fingers stuck together! They were stickier than I expected." At the sight the man exclaimed:

"God bless you, sir! I wish to give you something. Do you like oranges?"

"Sometimes."

He went to a shelf that was full of them and began to fill a great bag.

After he had put in a dozen or so Gough said, "That's enough."

But the man paid no attention, and went on filling the bag. Then he put it in Gough's arms, and said:

" There! don't say a word; but go along.
God bless you! "

Gough, in telling the story, said, " I
had positively to hire a cab to take me
home."

The later years of Mr. Gough were happy
and prosperous. They did not make him
proud, or rob him of his kindness of heart.
When Joel Stratton, the man whose touch
on the arm that October Sunday afternoon
had meant salvation to him, died, leaving his
family in financial straits, Gough counted it
a privilege to settle an annuity of three
hundred dollars upon his widow, which he
paid as regularly as the date recurred during her life.

John B. Gough left in the world a rare
fragrance of loving service rendered the
poor and the despairing, to whom he had
been as the angel of God. There were
thousands of others in the world, who felt
about him as the English woman did, who
brought a faded handkerchief to Mrs.
Gough, and said:

" I am very poor. I would give your husband a thousand pounds if I had it—I can only give him this (presenting the handkerchief). I married with the fairest prospects before me, but my husband took to drinking, and everything went, until, at last, I found myself in one miserable room. My husband lay drunk in the corner, and my sick child lay moaning on my knee. I wet this handkerchief with my tears. My husband met yours. He spoke a few words, and gave a grasp of the hand; and now for six years my husband has been all to me that a husband can be to a wife. I have brought your husband the very handkerchief I wet that night with my tears, and I want him to remember that he has wiped away those tears from my eyes, I trust forever." Years afterward speaking of that handkerchief Gough said:

" You do not think it worth three cents, but you have not money enough to buy it from me. These are the things that make men glad." Few men have had so much

of that gladness as did John B. Gough.   Oh
God! give us an army of earnest-souled and
loving-hearted men and women, who shall
seek their gladness in thus wiping away the
tears of the sorrowing!

FRANCES WILLARD AND THE
WHITE RIBBON MOVEMENT

When God lets loose an idea upon this planet we vainly set limits to its progress; and I believe that Gospel Temperance shall yet transform that inmost circle, the human heart, and in its widening sweep the circle of the home, and then society, and then pushing its argument to the extreme conclusion, it shall permeate the widest circle of them all, and that is, government.— FRANCES E. WILLARD.

CHAPTER VII

FRANCES WILLARD AND THE WHITE RIBBON MOVEMENT

ONE evening in the week before Christmas, 1873, Dr. Dio Lewis, a distinguished physician, and a popular lyceum lecturer of the time, delivered a lecture in Hillsboro, Ohio, on " Our Girls." He had come to the town under an engagement by the Lecture Association to fill only a single evening in the winter lecture course for the entertainment of the people; but as he happened to have no engagement for the next evening, some earnest spirits persuaded him to remain over in Hillsboro and deliver a free lecture on the subject of temperance.

Dr. Lewis was entertained in the home of Judge Thompson; but Mrs. Thompson had been unable to attend the lecture that evening because of the pressing nature of her household duties. Her son, a youth of sixteen, was present, however, and after the lecture, greatly excited about what had transpired, he related to his mother that Dr. Lewis had said that his own mother, and several of her good Christian friends, had united in prayer with and for the liquor sellers of his native town, until they had given up their soul-destroying business, and then had said, "Ladies, you might do the same thing in Hillsboro if you had the same faith"; and, turning to the ministers and temperance men who were upon the platform, added, "Suppose I ask the ladies of this audience to signify their opinions upon the subject?" As they all seemed pleased with the idea, he called on the women who were in favor of such action to rise, and fifty or more women had stood up in token of approval. He then asked the men how many of them would stand to back up the women if they should undertake the work; and some sixty or seventy had arisen. "And now, mother," said the enthusiastic boy,

" they have got you into business, for you are on a committee to do some work at the Presbyterian church in the morning at nine o'clock, and then the ladies want you to go out with them to the saloons."

Judge Thompson had that evening returned from court in another county, and, being very tired, was resting on the sofa, and the mother and her son, supposing that he was asleep, had been speaking in an undertone; but as the boy spoke about his mother going to the saloons, the Judge suddenly roused up, and exclaimed, " What tomfoolery is all that? " The boy slipped out of the room, and went to bed, while Mrs. Thompson assured her husband that she would not be led into any foolish act by Dr. Dio Lewis or anybody else. After he had relaxed into a milder mood, though continuing to scoff at the whole plan as " tomfoolery," the good woman ventured to remind him that the men had been in the " tomfoolery " business a long time, and suggested that it might be " God's will " that the women should now take their part.

The next morning, after breakfast, when they were gathered in the sitting-room, her son came up, and laying his hand on his mother's shoulder, inquired, " Mother, are you not going over to the church this morning?" As she hesitated, and doubtless showed in her countenance that she was greatly perplexed, the boy said, " But, my dear mother, you know you have to go." Then her daughter, who was sitting on a stool at her side, leaned over in a most tender manner, and looking up in her face, said, " Don't you think you will go?"

While this conversation had been going on, Judge Thompson had been walking the floor in silence. Suddenly he stopped, and placing his hand upon the family Bible that lay upon his wife's work-table, he said, " Children, you know where your mother goes to settle all vexed questions. Let us leave her alone." As he ceased speaking he walked out of the room, and the children followed. Mrs. Thompson turned the key in the lock, and was in the act of kneeling down to pray when she heard a gentle tap at the door. Upon opening it, she found her daughter with her Bible open, and the tears coursing down her cheeks as she said, " I opened to this, mother; it must be for you." She immediately left the room, and her mother sat down to read with new insight the wonderful message of promise in the One Hundred and Forty-sixth Psalm. It seemed a new psalm to her as she read:

" Put not your trust in princes, nor in the son of man, in whom there is no help. . . Happy is he that hath the God of Jacob for his help, whose hope is in the Lord his God: which made heaven, and earth, the sea, and all that therein is: which keepeth truth forever: which executeth judgment for the oppressed: which giveth food to the hungry. The Lord looseth the prisoners: the Lord openeth the eyes of the blind: the Lord raiseth them that are bowed down: the Lord loveth the righteous: the Lord preserveth the strangers; he relieveth the fatherless and the widow: but the way of the wicked he turneth upside down."

Doubting no longer what her duty was, she at once went to the Presbyterian church, where quite a large congregation had already gathered. She was at once unanimously chosen as the President; Mrs. General McDowell, Vice-president; and Mrs. D. K. Finner, Secretary, of the unique work which they were to perform.

They drew up appeals to druggists, saloon-keepers, and hotel proprietors. Then Dr. McSurely, the Presbyterian minister, who had up to this time occupied the chair, called upon the new president to come forward and take her place. She tried to get up; but, having never done any public work, her limbs refused to act, and she sat still. Wise Dr. McSurely looked around at the men and said, "Brethren, I see that the ladies will do nothing while we remain; let us adjourn, leaving this new work with God and the women."

After the men had filed out, and the door was closed behind them, new strength seemed to come to Mrs. Thompson; and she walked forward to the minister's table, took the large Bible, and, opening it, told the story of the morning's conversation and experiences in her own home. After she had read the psalm brought to her notice by her daughter, and had tearfully commented on it, she called upon Mrs. McDowell to lead in prayer. Now, Mrs. McDowell, though a good Christian woman for many years, had never in all her life heard her own voice in prayer; but she prayed that morning as though Isaiah's " coal of fire " had unsealed her lips.

As they rose from their knees, the President asked Mrs. Cowden, the wife of the Methodist minister, to lead in the singing of the old hymn " Give to the winds thy fears"; and turning to the rest of the women she said, "As we all join in singing this hymn, let us form in line, two and two, the small women in front, leaving the tall ones to bring up in the rear, and let us at once proceed to our sacred mission, trusting alone in the God of Jacob." As they marched out through the door of the church into the street, they were singing these prophetic words:

> " Far, far above thy thought,
> His counsels shall appear,
> When fully he the work hath wrought
> That caused thy needless fear."

They went to drug stores and saloons and hotels; they pleaded and sung and prayed, until saloon after saloon was closed at their entreaties. It was a divine contagion that spread throughout the land. In hundreds of towns and villages, from one ocean to the other, Christian women followed their example. Sometimes they were abused and mobbed; in some places they were arrested and thrown into jail; but it was a divine work; God was in it, and great good was accomplished.

Out of this wonderful upheaval, known as

the "Woman's Crusade," the Woman's Christian Temperance Union came into being, with its pledges and its bows of white ribbon. For years there had been growing in Illinois a farmer's girl, clean and wholesome and strong. She had been educated, not only in college, but by travel and hard work as a teacher, for the very purpose of this providential hour. So at the birth of the great woman's movement, stood Frances Willard, destined to become "the best loved woman" of the nineteenth century in America.

The spirit with which Frances Willard came to the leadership of the Woman's Christian Temperance Union is clearly illustrated in her first great "Home Protection" address. In the course of that eloquent discussion, she said:

"The strong-hold of the rum power lies in the fact that it has upon its side two deeply rooted appetites, namely: in the dealer, the appetite for gain, and in the drinker, the appetite for stimulants. We have dolorously said in times gone by that on the human plane we have nothing adequate to match against this frightful pair. But let us think more carefully, and we shall find that, as in nature God has given us an antidote to every poison, and in grace a compensation for every loss; so in human society, he has prepared against alcohol, that worst foe of the social state, an enemy under whose weapons it is to bite the dust.

" Think of it! There is a class in every one of our communities—in many of them far the most numerous class—which (I speak not vauntingly, but name it as a fact) has not, in all the centuries of wine, beer, and brandy drinking, developed, as a class, an appetite for alcohol, but whose instincts, on the contrary, set so strongly against intoxicants that if the liquor traffic were dependent on their patronage alone, it would collapse this night as if all the nitro-glycerine of Hell Gate reef had exploded under it.

" There is a class whose instinct of self-preservation must forever be opposed to a stimulant which nerves with dangerous strength arms already so much stronger than their own, and so maddens the brain God meant to guide those arms that they strike down the wives men love, and the little children for whom, when sober, they would die. The wife, largely dependent for the support of herself and little ones upon the brain which strong-drink paralyzes, the arm it masters, and the skill it renders futile, will, in the nature of the case, prove herself unfriendly to the actual or potential source of so much misery. But besides this primal instinct of self-preservation, we have in the same class of which I speak, another far more high and sacred—I mean the instinct of a mother's love, a wife's devotion, a sister's faithfulness, a daughter's loyalty. And now I ask you to consider earnestly the fact that none of these blessed rays of light and power from woman's heart are as yet brought to bear upon the rum shop at the focus of power.

They are, I know, the sweet and pleasant sunshine of our homes; they are the beams which light the larger home of social life, and send their gentle radiance out even into the great and busy world.

" But I know, and as the knowledge has grown clearer, my heart has thrilled with gratitude and hope too deep for words, that in a republic all these now divergent beams of light can, through that magic lens, that powerful sun-glass which we name the ballot, be made to converge upon the rum shop in a blaze of light that shall reveal its full abominations, and a white flame of heat which, like a pitiless moxa, shall burn this cancerous excrescence from America's fair form. Yes, for there is nothing in the universe so sure, so strong, as love; and love shall do all this—the love of maid for sweetheart, wife for husband, of a sister for her brother, of a mother for her son."

Frances Willard was one of the greatest and most persuasive orators that has ever appeared among women. The Rev. Dr.

Frank W. Gunsaulus, himself an orator of world-wide repute, pays a very beautiful tribute to her marvelous power on the platform. He comments on the fact that Miss Willard did not possess the splendid physical presence which in Mrs. Livermore—a speaker she never ceased to admire—has bent the bow of Ulysses with a superb and queenly ease. But when the bow-string twanged, which her fingers had touched, an arrow sped, as sharply tipped, as finely feathered, as sure to hit the object aimed at, as though the speaker had been of enormous frame, and breathed through a pair of organ-like lungs. " Indeed," says Gunsaulus, " students of oratory will agree that the wonder of Miss Willard's physical constitution, as compared with the amount of work which she performed, and the achievements she wrought as a public speaker, passed strangely out of sight when she exercised upon her audience the charm of her mellow and finely cadenced voice, attuned to the strenuous rhythm of her thought and feeling. When asked if she were a very large woman, an old toper, who was also a great lawyer, said, in describing her speech of the night before: 'I should think her about eight feet high, and weighing about four hundred pounds avoirdupois; but when she was wooing my heart to a better life, I thought then, and think now, that she was the sweetest little being in the world.' When an audience of six thousand had assembled together, and Miss Willard had serious arguments to plead, and something of a prejudice to overcome by battling for a position to which even the majority of her sisters had not assented, one wished she had more of brawny stoutness. When the harp trembled and shook with emotion, as she spoke of what she meant to do by the grace of God and by the force of strength that night, we feared that the strings might be worn away, and the echoing harmony be heard vanishingly; but as the eye lit up with hitherto unseen fire, the finely mobile lips moved with great messages so easily,

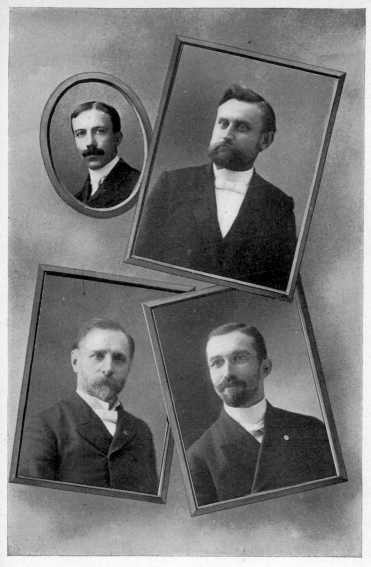

Wayne B. Wheeler, Esq.   Rev. P. A. Baker.
Rev. J. C. Jackson.   Rev. E. C. Dinwiddie.

GROUP FROM THE EARLY WORKING FORCE OF THE
ANTI-SALOON LEAGUE.

the chest expanded from slightness to large-
ness and strength proportionate to the rich-
ness of the outpouring truth, the most af-
fectionate and anxious friend felt supreme
confidence in the strength of her nerves and
the boundlessness of her vital energy, and
nothing seemed able to tire or to vanquish
that combination of powers which was il-
luminated by the vast reserve of spiritual
power attending her progress.   To hear her,
after the massive speech of even a more
ponderous brain to whom auditors gave
shouts of approval, was like listening to
Wendell Phillips, calm, yet fiery, alert, yet
serenely sure of the truth, while yet the
magnificent excitement and stalwart glory
of Daniel Webster made the air tremble and
burn."   Henry Ward Beecher declared that
no woman of her day more truly illustrated
the fact that forcefulness and influence for
good can be obtained only by the alliance of
a clear head and a warm heart in public
than did Frances Willard.   " I always feel,"
said he, " that she might inundate the whole

assembly with tears if she were not so wise, and that she might take us to heights of reasoning where we would all freeze to death, if she were not so kind."

John Greenleaf Whittier once said of Miss Willard what was perhaps as splendid a characterization as was ever uttered: " I always want to tell her ' Thee must know thee is great only as thy cause makes thee great. Thee might be only a lot of good qualities if they had not been fused.' " But by the fiat of God they were fused to white heat, and they burned their way into the hearts of the world. Under her leadership the Woman's Christian Temperance Union bound its bows of ribbon white around the world, printed its pledges in all the tongues spoken by civilized peoples, and presented to mankind the spectacle of the largest organization formed by women since the world began, consecrated to total abstinence and to conflict with the liquor traffic.

FRANCIS MURPHY AND HIS
COLLEAGUES

The reclaiming power of love is great; aye, it is powerful; yea, it is most potent. I know this, for I have seen the most degraded taken from the very gutter. It pays to be kind, it pays to be merciful. Speak the kind word; perform the kind act. It may be your passport to eternal bliss.— FRANCIS MURPHY.

CHAPTER VIII

FRANCIS MURPHY in 1873 was in jail for illegal liquor selling in Portland, Maine. While there Captain Cyrus Sturdivant, a man of faith, asked the sheriff for permission to come and talk with the prisoners. Murphy thus writes of their first meeting:

" To Captain Sturdivant, if I have been of any use in the world, under God, I owe all of it. He commenced his work on the Sabbath day. The great, dark entrance door was opened to the Christian people. Quite a number had collected together, and they came in singing, 'All hail the power of Jesus' name'; I was sitting on the little iron bedstead in my cell, when the keeper came to the door, and looking at me, said:

" ' Mr. Murphy, we would like to have

157

you come out and attend religious services.'

"'Please excuse me; I will remain here, and not disturb your people,' was my prompt reply.

"'Come out; these people are your friends; they will not injure you,' persisted the keeper.

"There was something so kind and agreeable in the face of the man, that it produced a disposition of assent within me, and touched my heart.   Yet my answer was:

"'I would sooner stay here.'

"'Come on, Mr. Murphy,' he continued.

"At this, I concluded I would go.   Oh, how my heart had ached for a kind word; for someone to say, 'Can I do anything for you?'   I then responded:

"'I will go out with you, I believe.'

"I rose from my seat, stepped out of the little open door, walked about ten paces, and sat down with the rest of the prisoners. There was Captain Cyrus Sturdivant.   His back was turned toward me as I walked

along the corridor. When he turned about,
he was weeping as a mother sometimes
weeps for her child. As I looked at his
face, I asked myself, ' Who is he weeping
for; has he lost a son?' No, it was evident
that he had a heart for others. He was
telling of God's goodness. His words were
very sweet to me. He spoke to us of hungry
wives and children. And, at that moment,
it seemed I could see my poor wife and
children before me. As he continued to
talk, it semed to me that my imagination
never realized so powerfully as it did at
that time, the presence of the objects of my
affections. My children seemed to be about
me; and my dear wife was standing in my
presence, as calm and patient as ever, saying not one word. I queried, ' Does anyone
care for me? I wonder if there is a
friendly hand here to be extended to me?'
And I said to myself, ' Oh, what would I
not give to sit down with that man and tell
him the sorrow of my heart!' ' "

Captain Sturdivant followed the matter

up until Murphy was happily converted to Christ, and with it, of course, came his determination to cease to have anything to do with intoxicating drinks. He remained a prisoner for some time afterwards, and his work as a reformer began during his prison days.

One day he conceived a project of carrying the work begun in his own soul, among the unconverted men around him. He sent a petition to the sheriff, asking his permission to hold a prayer-meeting. The meeting was held, and was one of powerful influence for good. In the course of a little time, he saw the seventy-five men in the jail brought securely from the evil of their lives. God gave him every man in the jail. Murphy took this as a sign from God that henceforth he was to give himself to the work of rescuing and reforming his fellow-men. The result was so wonderful in the conduct of the men that the sheriff discontinued the practice of locking them up. They were put upon their honor. Contrary to the previous custom of the place, they were permitted to go out into the yard, and not one of them ever violated his word to the keeper.

Francis Murphy delivered his first lecture in the City Hall, Portland, Maine, April 3, 1873. The success was remarkable. A great crowd was present, and the humor and pathos of the discourse captivated the audience. That very evening he received over sixty applications for lectures in other cities. He was already launched upon his career. From Maine he went to New Hampshire, and then to Iowa and Illinois, and then to all the world.

Francis Murphy was very remarkable for the number of drinking men of great prominence and influence whom he won to sobriety through personal and individual work, in addition to the multitudes who were persuaded to take the pledge at his public meetings. This cannot be better illustrated than to give a condensed quotation from one of Murphy's speeches, delivered in Columbus, Ohio. He said:

"Allow me to use an illustration that I may enforce this truth, and may God help me. I will speak of a man you have had in your midst speaking for you—Marshall Swartzwalder. He was a victim of this habit for a number of years. He is a perfect gentleman when he is sober, a kingly man, and has justly been called the patriarch of the Pittsburg Bar, and the Demosthenes of the profession. Perhaps no man who has been upon the platform in the cause of human reform has been equal to him. When I first came to the city of Pittsburg, I was told about Marshall Swartzwalder that he had been a drunkard a great many years— for thirty years at least—and they said there was no hope for him. I said I would like to see him. ' Well,' said they, ' you can see him,' but said that he had been on a tremendous spree. I got the number of his office—for at this time he stayed in his office, and ate his meals there, and had a nice back room handsomely furnished where he slept—I rapped at his door; there was a young boy, a son of his, a beardless boy, about sixteen years of age, that always stayed with his father and never left him; he called him Dick. Dick came to the door —I wish you could have seen the poor boy; he looked so depressed and sad. Said I, 'Is Mr. Swartzwalder in?' He replied, 'Yes; do you wish to see him?' He sent in my card. He had asked what my name was, and stepped in and told him that Mr. Murphy was in the office and would like to see him. Said he, 'Send him in; I would like to see him.' So I went to his room, and he rose from his large chair, which he had for his own comfort. He extended his hand, and said, 'You're the man that has been talking temperance here?' 'Yes,' said I. 'Well, said he, 'we never have much good from you temperance people; you come here and sing your songs, and present your bills, and go away. That is the way they do, and I suppose you are like all the rest of them.' I said, 'I don't know how that is.' He said, 'Mr. Murphy, I want to talk to you. I have been a victim of intemperance for more than thirty years. I have no power to control myself.' He asked me to be seated in a chair, and I sat down by his side. He looked strangely in my face, and said, ' Is there any hope for me?' Said I, ' There is hope for you.' ' There is?' he exclaimed. ' Yes.' ' How so?' Said I, ' With God's help you can be saved.' With a shake of his head, he said, ' Why, for more than twenty years I have been seeking for the truth, and have read the Bible through and through. And,' said he, ' Mr. Murphy, there is no help for me.' I commenced talking to him in my humble way, the best I could. He turned around to Colonel Hetherington, and said: ' Go and tell Dick to come in.' The dear boy, when he came in, stepped up to his father's left side, and the father put his arms around the boy. The poor boy was so much overcome that he sat down and put his arms around his father's neck. The child could not control his feelings, and commenced to weep. The father said: ' Dear Dick, you

never left me.' Turning to me, he said:
' Mr. Murphy, here is a boy that stays with
his father; here is a boy that has walked the
streets night after night for his father, and
stays with him; I wish I could tell you how
good he has been, how much I love him.'
Before we got through talking to each other,
Mr. Swartzwalder said: ' Mr. Murphy, I
feel a very strange impression on my heart, I
feel as though God had touched me, so to
speak.' I said to him, with all the power of
encouragement that God had possessed me
with, ' Mr. Swartzwalder, by the grace of
God, you shall conquer this evil; I know it
in my heart.' I left him; I knew the work
was done; I knew it was a question of time
when the man should come out redeemed."
And indeed he was wonderfully redeemed,
and Murphy tells us that twenty thousand
men signed the pledge under the influence
of that one man. That story is typical of a
great many that might be told of Francis
Murphy.

The Murphy movement was distinguished

on the part of its followers by the wearing of a bit of blue ribbon in the button-hole of the coat, and so rapidly did the movement spread that the blue ribbon became a well-known badge from one ocean to the other. The work in some cities was phenomenal. Eighty thousand signed the Murphy pledge in Pittsburg. One hundred and twenty thousand signed the pledge in Philadelphia within two months, and in the State of Pennsylvania alone four hundred thousand wore the blue ribbon.

Dr. Henry A. Reynolds was in the city of Bangor, Maine, on the verge of delirium tremens. In his despair of human aid he knelt in his office, and yielded himself to God as his servant, and swore a solemn and sacred oath that he would sign the pledge publicly on the first opportunity. Two days later the opportunity came. The Woman's Crusade, of Bangor, was conducting a public meeting in the City Hall, and he went in to observe it.

The large audience was much amazed to

see him come in, for he was notorious for his intemperate habits. The people were more amazed when he pressed his way through the mass, and reached the pledge table, where he deliberately signed his name. The audience burst forth into enthusiastic cheers.

A little later he published notices in the different daily newspapers, cordially inviting all drinking men to meet at a certain time and place. Eleven came forward at the call, and the Bangor Reform Club, the very first of the kind, was organized September 10, 1874, adopting as its motto, "Dare to do right." Dr. Reynolds was elected President. Meetings were frequently held, and as each member sought after others, in the course of a few weeks, the club numbered hundreds, and the city was shaken and aroused for God and humanity as never before. The movement went over the country like a flash, creating great surprise and great interest. During the first year, reform clubs of this kind were organized throughout the entire State of Maine. In three years the number of reformed men was given as forty-six thousand.

The origin of the red ribbon took place some months after Dr. Reynolds' conversion. He had called a convention of reformed men to meet in Bangor, Maine, and while he was seated in his office, he fancied that it would be a good idea if the men had some sign or badge by which they could recognize each other. He thought for a long time, and finally sent his office boy across the street to a dry-goods store for several yards of red ribbon. Having obtained this, the doctor cut it up into six-inch lengths, tied one in the lapel of his coat, and did likewise by all the delegates. Dr. Reynolds was soon invited to other States, and it was not long before it spread over many States, doing a large amount of good. Space fails us to tell of P. A. Burdick, Thomas Doutney, Lou Beauchamp, and a vast host of others who have sought through the temper-

ance pledge to rouse the hope in the drunkard's heart of a possible rescue, and to
strengthen the purpose, and give solidity to
the will of the young and innocent, so as to
give them strength to resist the temptations
of the insidious foe.

HOWARD H. RUSSELL, ORGANIZER
OF THE ANTI-SALOON LEAGUE

With public sentiment nothing can fail, without it nothing can succeed. Consequently he who molds public sentiment goes deeper than he who enacts statutes or pronounces decisions. He makes statutes or decisions possible or impossible to be executed.—ABRAHAM LINCOLN.

CHAPTER IX

HOWARD H. RUSSELL, ORGANIZER OF THE
ANTI-SALOON LEAGUE

HOWARD H. RUSSELL, the founder
of the Ohio Anti-Saloon League, and
superintendent from the beginning, of both
State and National Leagues, and in whose
fertile brain was conceived the idea of The
Lincoln Legion, is of English ancestry.
His grandfather, James Russell, a skilled
iron-worker at Wednesbury, in Staffordshire, England, brought his family to Philadelphia in 1820, and Russell's father was
born there in 1822. The grandfather, for
forty years, was a foreman of Government
gun-makers at Harper's Ferry, Virginia,
and Springfield, Massachusetts. Howard's
father, Joseph A. Russell, sought an
education, worked his own way, was
graduated at the Wesleyan Academy, at

Wilbraham, Massachusetts, and the Episcopal Theological Seminary of Alexandria,
Virginia. Howard's mother was Sarah E.
Parker, a Dalton, Massachusetts, girl, a
daughter of the Revolution. The father
was a Home Missionary under Bishop
Kemper at Stillwater, Minnesota, when
Howard Russell was born there on Sunday
morning, October 21, 1855. The father's life
work was that of teacher as well as clergy-
man. He was principal of the Glens Falls,
New York, Academy, in the sixties, and had
charge of public and church schools in
Illinois and Iowa for nearly forty years.
After a very useful career, he still lives as
Rector Emeritus of the Episcopal Church at
Chariton, Iowa.

Howard Russell's boyhood was spent at
Bloomsburg, Pennsylvania, where his
mother died when he was six years of age,
and at Glens Falls, New York, where the
father was married a second time to a noble
woman who proved to be, to Howard and his
two brothers, a faithful and beloved second

mother, who still lives to bless the father in his old age. Young Russell studied at Galva, Illinois, and at Davenport, Iowa, where he finished preparatory school at Griswold College in 1872. Four summers of this time were spent working upon the farm. At seventeen years of age he was for a time clerk in the Commanding Officer's office at Rock Island Arsenal, then his friend Lieutenant Wright placed him in charge of the construction work at the Government waterpower dam at Moline.

In 1874, before Russell was nineteen, he crossed the plains in the saddle, with a cattle herd, secured a teacher's certificate in Colorado, and taught a few months near Hughes' Station, now Brighton, Colorado, then returning to his father's home at Corning, Iowa, where he took charge of a country paper for a year. Then at the age of twenty-one he began the study of law at Corning with the Hon. Frank M. Davis, teaching school the while at Noda-away, Iowa, to pay expenses. Later he

worked his way through a year at the Des
Moines Law School, and in June, 1878, was
admitted to the Bar before the Supreme
Court of Iowa. In 1880, Howard H. Russell married Lillian Davis, the daughter of
his preceptor and partner. She had already been for several years an inspiration
to his life.

Russell's six years as a lawyer were
very active ones. Mr. Davis received him
as a partner as soon as he was admitted
to the bar, and, as Davis was one of the
ablest lawyers in the State, and had already
the largest practice of any attorney in the
county, the young man did not lack for
work. He took part, not only in the civil,
but in the criminal practice. Early in his
experience as a lawyer he was employed to
defend a Corning druggist named William
Kline, who was charged with a murder
which had been committed a hundred miles
away, near Des Moines. Detectives had
conspired for the sake of a large reward to
fasten the crime upon Russell's client, who

was an innocent man.   Three different persons swore that Kline had confessed the murder.   Others testified that he was near the scene of the murder when he claimed to have been far away.   Several citizens of Corning, with book entries of business transactions with the defendant, established a conclusive alibi.   It was an exciting case. As it was tried at the State Capital, it attracted wide attention, and, as Russell won the victory single-handed against lawyers of large experience, it opened the way to rapid business success.   He also won many important civil cases while he was in the practice.   His last lawsuit was a civil damage suit against a liquor dealer on behalf of a wife who had been injured by the sale of liquor to her husband, and the jury gave a large verdict.   There is no doubt that had Russell remained at the law, he would have won honor and large financial return.

In 1882, through the prayers and influence of his devoted wife, he experienced a thorough change of heart motives, and under the new impulses then potent with him, was impelled toward the Christian ministry. This step was hastened by a political defeat. It had been the practice for years in Adams County, Iowa, to elect a young lawyer as County Superintendent of Schools. He was expected only to devote a part of his time to that work. In 1881, Russell was elected to that position, and served two years. In the summer of 1883 he was renominated by the Republican County Convention, but a fusion of the Democrats and "Greenbackers" defeated the whole Republican ticket that year, and though he received more votes than any other candidate of his party, he was still defeated by a narrow margin. Russell has since recognized that this defeat was a blessing in disguise, for it speeded his career into Christian and reform work. In the autumn of 1883 he closed up his business, and, with his wife and little daughter, Julia, two years of age, went to Oberlin, Ohio, and began his college and seminary studies January 1, 1884. In 1886 he won the

HOWARD H. RUSSELL,

Organizer of the Anti-Saloon League.

oratorical contest at Oberlin on the subject
of " Mob and Law," and represented Oberlin at the State contest, winning the first
place there. At the Interstate Contest at
Lawrence, Kansas, he represented Ohio, and
was awarded the second prize. In June,
1888, he had nearly finished his college
course, had completed his seminary course,
and was graduated from the theological department. In 1894 he was honored with the
degree of Master of Arts by Oberlin College,
and in 1897 the degree of Doctor of Divinity
was conferred upon him by the Ohio Wesleyan University.

During his student days at Oberlin, Russell had been preaching all the while, and
had been successful in bringing about revivals in religion in North and South Amherst. On his graduation he moved at once
to Kansas City, Missouri, to take up work
under the Congregational City Missionary
Society.

Russell began his ministry in Kansas
City in a huge tent, which he set up upon

vacant lots in the southwest part of the city.
He published a paper, *The Southwest Work-
man,* and distributed large editions among
the homes. By thorough advertising and
private canvass from house to house and
heart-winning sermons, he gathered great
congregations which he took into a large
hall nearby when the cold weather came.
The Sunday-school grew until it enrolled
five hundred. A temperance society and
young people's society, a boys' battalion
of two companies, were organized, and then
a church. A commodious building was
erected, and in two and a half years the
church came to be self-supporting. A revival added over one hundred members
one winter.

During the summer months each year
Russell supplied the pulpit of the First
Congregational Church, of which the Rev.
Dr. Henry Hopkins was pastor. The
second summer he preached a series of discourses upon the general topic of " A Lawyer's Examination of the Bible." A special

invitation was sent by the officers of the
church to lawyers and their families. There
was a large attendance of men of that profession, and a high degree of interest manifested. Lengthy reports of the addresses
were printed in the Kansas City papers, and
he received letters from five lawyers residing
in towns of Kansas and Missouri who were
led to unite with the Church from reading
those reports. One hundred business men
in Kansas City, Kansas, signed a request for
the delivery of these addresses, and presented Russell with a generous purse at the
closing service. This series of discourses
was printed in a handsome volume by the
Fleming H. Revell Company, and has
reached a fourth edition. While in Kansas
City, in 1889, Ernest Clement, a son, was
born to the Russells.

In November, 1890, Philip Armour sent
a committee to visit the Southwest Tabernacle, and soon a call came to Russell to the
pastorate of the Armour Mission in Chicago,
and as that promised a wider opportunity

for effective work, he began service there in
February, 1891. Here was room for work,
indeed! The Sunday-school enrolled over
two thousand members, and the Mission,
through its kindergarten, free dispensary,
and other helpful agencies, touched in various ways a parish of four or five thousand
people. Russell's pastoral work there, while
burdensome, was very delightful. He organized, while there, a brotherhood for the
young men, a sisterhood for the young
women, and a battalion for the boys. There
were five companies of boys, over two hundred and fifty in line, and, with their blue
uniforms and guns, they presented a fine appearance. Best of all, they were induced,
most of them, to become soldiers of Christ.
More than a hundred and fifty of them in a
single winter intelligently enlisted in Christian service. W. C. Johnson, a faithful
Christian worker, who had drilled Russell's
boy battalion in Kansas City, came at his
call, to Chicago, and was his stenographer
and assistant pastor. The remarkable fea-

ture of the case was, that these boys themselves cheerfully paid the assistant's salary.

During Russell's pastorate at the Armour Mission, his sorrow and indignation were constantly stirred by the evils of the liquor habit and traffic, and it was here that the National Anti-Saloon League gained its great reserve of power.

In the granite hills of New Hampshire, looking down upon beautiful " Grafton Water," where Russell and the writer of this volume are summer neighbors and friends, I inquired of him how he came to take up the Anti-Saloon League work at so large a cost in personal sacrifice, both for himself and for his family, also expressing wonder that I had never seen anything in print concerning it. Thus urged, he told me this story:

" While convalescing from a long illness at the Armour Mission, in the fall of 1892, it came to me vividly that I ought to take up the marshaling of the church forces of the country to do active and permanent service against the saloon. I had long believed it ought to be done, and I had tried to induce others to take it up. I had even offered to contribute $100 per year out of my salary, if a friend would take the lead in the work. Mary Lyon once said: 'If there is work which needs the doing, and no one else will do it, and I can do it, that is my work.' Now, it seemed to come to me that this work which so much needed the doing, and which I had several times sought to lay upon others, was the very work I ought to set in upon. I shrank from it still. I had been blessed in my pastoral work. It would break up the home life. Would the people of the churches support the many workers needed to do an effective work, and the other necessary expenses? As at other times in my life, God at last made it clear that I was no longer to hesitate or shrink from it. Happily the path of duty seemed plain to Mrs. Russell also, and then I set about finding where I was to begin the task. It was reported that citizens of Indiana were looking for a man to lead their temperance work, and I went

to Indianapolis, but found that they were
not ready to take up the lines of work I had
in mind, so I turned again to my Oberlin
friends. They were at first reluctant to assume responsibility in the matter, but after
deliberation and prayer, and several conferences with the pastors and other leaders,
in the spring of 1893, they consented to
adopt my ideas and plans, and to help as
much as they could to start the work and to
give it their permanent assistance. The public beginning was made at a Union Meeting
at the First Congregational Church at Oberlin, on Sunday evening, June 4, 1893.

"My life the past ten years has been
entirely absorbed with the life and growth
of the Anti-Saloon League. In September,
1893, my family came from Chicago, and we
rented a small house at $10 per month in
the northern part of Columbus. Knowing
the financial difficulties sure to be encoun-
tered, Mrs. Russell dismissed her maid and
bravely did all the housework herself. The
home sacrifices and burdens connected with

the initiation of this League work were more
than will ever be known. When anyone
gives me flowers because of my work as a
temperance leader, I present them all to my
dear wife, who, no less surely because out
of public view, has furnished the inspiration and put up the prayers, and given the
personal sacrifices and toil which supplied
our partnership in service its best essentials
for success. Let us never forget the costly
part womanhood pays in the advancement of
this reform. As the lady bravely buckled on
the armor of her knight and cheered him on
to the battle even when her heart was break-
ing, so the heroic comrade of my home has
cheered me forth to the conflicts of the last
decade, and has never wavered in her faith
and loyalty to the duties which attended or
grew out of the commission. Several hundred dollars of her patrimony were freely
spent in the early years of our struggle to
hold a footing for the League, during the
hard times the whole nation saw, from 1893
to 1896. The children, too, have had their

part in the sacrifices of this reform work.
How often the tears of parting have fallen
as the father went forth for his long ab-
sences. When Ernest was six years old,
he said to me sadly one day, at Columbus:
' Papa, why do you go away so far to fight
saloons? There are some right up here on
the street. You can stay home with us and
fight them!' "

Three years the Russells lived in Columbus, and nearly six in Delaware, Ohio, and
then, for the sake of the daughter's post-
graduate study, their residence was for
nearly two years in Boston, and they removed to New York City in June, 1903.

Professor W. F. Whitlock, D. D., of Delaware, Ohio, an old neighbor and friend of
Howard Russell's, in a keen analysis of his
character and personality, in connection
with the great work which he has done for
the temperance movement, gives it as his
judgment that as a reformer he is particu-
larly gifted in the following elements:

" First, in organizing ability. Given a

problem to solve his mind readily suggests a solution. When a campaign is to be made, he quickly conceives the plan. He is apt in collecting and combining the forces. He knows at once the point of attack, and concentrates everything upon it. The two things the temperance reform has lacked, organization and concentration, he happily commands. System, compactness, combination, concentration, are not sacrificed by him to mere sentiment or theory. He grasps not only the end, but the means that will reach it. His unfaltering faith is not a substitute for work, but is revealed and realized in his works.

"A second element is contained in his practical and workable methods. They are such as commend themselves to reason and sound judgment by the manifest adaptation of means to ends. He is never without a theory, but he is not a mere theorist. He is broad enough to face conditions as they are, without growing impatient because they are not as they ought to be. His methods are

determined upon in the light of two considerations: they must be honorable, authorized
by worthy features only, and then adapted
to the work attempted. His own self-reliant
convictions happily harmonize with sug-
gestions resulting from deliberations and
counsels. The inherent force of his proposed
plans and methods assures the friends and
alarms the foes of the cause he advocates.

" A third element is his faith in ultimate
success. He is a continual inspiration to
those associated in effort with him. He is
sure that his work is one that ought to be
done, and therefore can be. He never measures the promise of success or failure by the
number and force of the foe, but by the faith
and aggressive effort of professed friends.
He spends no time in complaining of the
past, but is eager to realize the possibilities
of the present. He is not a critic, much less
a faultfinder. He gladly recognizes the good
that has been done, and makes it the basis of
greater achievements. He is not a pessimist,
refusing to see the service others have ren-

dered; not a visionary optimist, anticipating
success without a struggle, but a knight of
cool judgment and steady nerve, ready for
the fray, and confident of the outcome.

" A fourth element is the moral and religious power put into the reform. He is
fully conscious that the work is of the Master, and must be done in His name. The
churches, the Sunday-schools, the young people's organizations, and all Christian asso-
ciations and leagues are enlisted. The Bible
is the guidebook, and Christians are the dis-
ciplined forces that must bring light and victory. His own earnest and eloquent appeals
are first of all to religious people. His belief
that his mission is divinely given, and the
burdensome yearning of his spirit pleading
in behalf of the wayward and unfortunate,
give a strange sacredness to the cause he rep-
resents. He is a man of one work, and his
consecration seems complete. The man, the
Christian, the lawyer, the minister, the
author, his talents and acquisitions, his
voice and pen, all that he is and has, are ab-

sorbed in his divinely appointed work. May the mightiness of his mission, his giant efforts, fervent faith, unflagging zeal, and earnest supplications be crowned with the ' unity, persistency, and victory ' of the hosts he leads ! "

In addition to this excellent analysis by Dr. Whitlock, to which I am ready heartily to subscribe, I wish to call attention to another characteristic, not always found in the reformer, but of the greatest possible value as a factor for practical work, and, that is, a well-balanced, sunny spirit, a sweetness of temper, a genuine loveableness of character which not only inspires respect and admiration, but which draws men to him in the bonds of sympathy and love. This is Howard H. Russell, whose name will be forever associated with the birth and development of the Anti-Saloon League movement, and whose head and heart are responsible for The Lincoln Legion. He is of his own age and time, a Reformer of the Twentieth Century. The same old enthusiasm, and fire, and spirit of self-sacrifice, but with characteristics modified to fit him to the new age in which his work is to be done. A well-balanced, thoroughly consecrated, devoted man, frank, genuine, whole-hearted, reverencing God, loving humanity, this is Howard H. Russell. God give strength to his arm, eloquence to his tongue, and patience to his heart for still mightier triumphs.

THE ANTI-SALOON LEAGUE

The temperance reform is not a weary journey to reach a destination. It is world-wide conflict against woe-working sin, and many splendid triumphs are already won. Let no man be discouraged. Trust thou in God, for we shall join yet more and more in jubilant praise, for His mighty salvation from the Satanic power of strong drink.— HOWARD H. RUSSELL.

CHAPTER X

THE ANTI-SALOON LEAGUE

ALL great movements have gathered about some distinct and typical personality. Emerson tells us that every great institution is but the lengthening shadow of a man. Mahomet stands for Mohammedism, Martin Luther for the Reformation, George Washington for the American Revolution, John Wesley for Methodism. When a great task is to be wrought out, God lays the burden of it upon some man's heart, and by inheritance and environment, as well as by discipline and culture, fits him for his work, and drives him forward by a divine impulse until it is accomplished.

The Anti-Saloon League, like every other institution that has been a force for good in the world, has been a growth, and has received into its life great personal sacrifice and service upon the part of many devoted people. While others deserve credit for valuable assistance and unselfish service, without which the results would have been impossible, it still remains true that one man conceived the plan of the organization, as it has finally crystallized into a working engine, without material change from the " pattern in the Mount." He saw the visions and dreamed the dreams. By faith he foresaw the coming constituency, the methods of work, and the sure victories of the movement. He was the first missionary in the new crusade utterly to put himself, and all he had, into it. He aroused the needed faith in others, raised the sinews of war, enlisted other leaders, mobilized the army, and conducted such victorious campaigns as have already won the respect of political powers, the fear of saloon-keepers and their allies, the rapidly growing support of all moral agencies, and made the organization a permanent factor in this " noblest conflict of the New Century."

Howard H. Russell, from early boyhood had distinct impressions of the evil of the drink habit and traffic. While yet a lad he saw near and dear relatives brought to a premature death through strong drink. It became evident to him that for several generations this habit had been a family weakness. When visiting recently in Staffordshire, England, Russell found that at least fourteen relatives not far removed, bright young men, several of them trained in the English universities, had all died before reaching forty years of age, and that the drink habit was the assassin in every case. It is no wonder that the subject was always in his mind as of pressing importance.

When a young lawyer in Iowa, his firm were employed by a local temperance organization to prosecute lawless saloon-keepers, and to Russell was assigned the prosecution of the cases. He thus learned the perjury and anarchy characterizing such traffickers. He was often called upon

for temperance addresses, and in 1883 he
devoted a month to the State Campaign for
a Prohibitory Amendment to the Iowa Constitution.

During his collegiate course at Oberlin
from 1884 to 1888, he was repeatedly
sent as a delegate to represent the
college at temperance conferences and
conventions. While a student, in 1885,
he led in the Murphy movement at
North Amherst and South Amherst, Ohio,
and again while still a seminarian at Oberlin, but residing at Berea, Ohio, and pastor
of the Berea Congregational Church, he
organized a local movement which closed
eight saloons, and they have remained
closed ever since. A vicious physical as-
sault upon him on the street, by a saloon-
keeper, helped to carry the election by six
majority.

When the saloon-keepers, thus legally
forced out of trade by the village ordinance,
continued to sell liquor in violation of law,
he secured abundance of evidence and began

the prosecutions, conducted the trials himself in the Mayor's Court, and secured such heavy penalties against the law-breakers that they were compelled to obey the law. When he left Berea to go to Kansas City in 1888, the citizens generally gave a Farewell Reception and a written testimonial with numerous signatures in recognition of his services in the temperance cause while a citizen of Berea.

In December, 1887, the Oberlin Temperance Alliance requested Mr. Russell to take charge of a movement to secure a needed law from the legislature. They offered to furnish $300 in money toward expenses, and to supply his Berea pulpit when it was necessary to be absent therefrom. He opened a headquarters at Columbus. By working through the pastors and churches a temporary "Local Option League," as it was called, was formed throughout the State and petitions were circulated in every county for the passage of the Township Local Option Bill. Pre-

viously, in 1886, the legislature in the enactment of the Dow Law had given the councils
of the various municipalities in the State
the power to regulate or prohibit the sale of
liquors as beverages. It was under that
provision that the Berea saloons were closed.
In many localities when the village council
closed the saloons they opened again for
business in the township just outside the
line. The enactment of the township local
option law was planned so as to enable the
farmers to protect the township from the
saloon and incidentally to protect the village or city voting out the saloons. Under
the pressure of the people stirred up by the
Local Option League, the bill was pushed
through the house by a small majority and
went over to the senate. Here a poll of the
senate made by Senator Park Alexander of
Akron, who was an earnest friend of the
bill, showed a bare majority of one in its
favor. On a certain Wednesday morning
the bill was to come to a vote. On Monday
morning, two days before, Senator Crook of

Dayton went to Senator Alexander and said that three committees of the brewers, distillers, and saloon-keepers of Dayton had called upon him the previous day and he felt that he must withdraw his promise to vote for the bill. Monday afternoon Mr. Russell went to Dayton, and through friends of the measure, secured the writing on Tuesday of many personal letters to Senator Crook. On Wednesday morning several telegrams were sent him and when the bill came up he voted for it and it was passed by a majority of one vote. Senator Alexander remarked afterward to Mr. Russell that the old prophecy of Isaiah had now been fulfilled: " The rough places shall be made plain, and the crooked places shall be made straight"! This township law, still an effective temperance measure in Ohio, was the entering wedge for local option laws in that State. By its use over 300 townships are kept free from saloons. This four-months' legislative experience led Mr. Russell to believe that a permanent organization of the temperance forces of the churches might make gradual and more rapid headway than hitherto in obtaining anti-saloon legislation. In making his final report to the Oberlin Temperance Alliance in April, 1888, Mr. Russell urged that the temporary organization be made permanent and that a salaried superintendent be employed to take charge of the work. A county organization was afterward formed in Lorain County and there the matter rested.

While pastor of the Southwest Tabernacle in Kansas City in 1890, Mr. Russell sent circular letters to the pastors throughout Missouri asking their opinion upon the subject, and as the result a largely attended convention was called, and held at Pertle Springs, Missouri, in July, 1890, and a constitution was adopted providing for work in the lines of agitation, law enforcement, and legislation by a State organization named the Missouri Anti-Liquor League. Mr. Russell was elected the President for the first year, and he gave his whole two months' vacation without charge to the League, presenting the work at various points in the State. The first fifty dollars expended in printing and postage in working up the State convention in Missouri were furnished by members of the Oberlin Temperance Alliance. Mr. W. J. Reese was appointed organizer, and with a stereopticon which Mr. Russell furnished him, he went out and organized leagues, some of which still continue their work. The State League temporarily ceased its work when Mr. Russell was called early in 1891 to take pastoral charge of the Armour Mission in Chicago. In 1892 Mr. Russell was invited to deliver a temperance address at Oberlin, and he again advocated the forming of a permanent State organization in Ohio, and tried to induce certain men to take charge of the work, but nothing was done. His pastoral work in Chicago brought before him many tragedies resulting from the drink. Standing upon a box at an undertaker's door, he conducted the funeral of a suicide through drink; the drunkard's home had gone and his weeping family sat within the door. Again it was the " only son of his mother, and she a widow," who had been wounded in a saloon brawl on Sunday and afterward died in the hospital. In another case it was the mother with seven sorrowing children who had died in childbirth after being brutally struck by her drunken husband. The doctor gave the man money to buy medicine for the wife and he bought whisky for himself, and on the day of the funeral lay drunk on the floor of the back room. Again it was a child driven forth by a drunken father to freeze to death.

In the fall of 1892, Mr. Russell talked privately with some of the Oberlin citizens again about the need of State organization in Ohio. They said, "If you will take charge of it, it might be made a success." There was a natural hesitation upon his part to leave the regular line of church work in which he was blessed, to be absent most of the time from his family. The question of support was utterly untried and uncertain. At the time of indecision a new tragedy stirred his heart. He was called as minister to a home where a drunken mother lay dead. The father was intoxicated, as were also the undertaker's driver and some neighbor women. The little boy of eight years and his little sister of three—worse than orphans —were the only unpolluted objects in the desolate room. " Do you know what caused your mother's death? " he asked. " I do. It was drink," said the weeping boy. " Are you going to drink? " " I'll never touch it! " He pledged the boy, whose clinched hand he raised, never to drink that which took his mother's life, and to teach his sister to do likewise. The next morning when he called, the house was vacant, and that home like so many others was broken up by rum! It was there and then he settled the question of his future work as a reformer. He said to himself, " I will go out to my brethren of the churches and demand that they become responsible for an organized

activity that shall hasten the day when that
kind of tragedies shall be done away."
There were two or three conferences at
Oberlin between January and May, 1893,
and at Mr. Russell's request the Oberlin
Temperance Alliance, at a meeting held in
the College Library on May 24, 1893, for-
mally voted to initiate and to stand
officially behind the movement until it
should be thought best to expand the work
into a State organization. It was voted at
that meeting that accounts should be
kept and money received and paid by the
Oberlin organization for the present,
and Mr. Russell was employed as Superintendent upon a definite salary to introduce
the movement to the people of the State,
and as rapidly as possible to organize and
federate the churches into a league against
the saloons according to plans he had out-
lined to the Alliance.

As had been voted at the Alliance meeting on May 24, the formal public beginning of the Anti-Saloon League was made

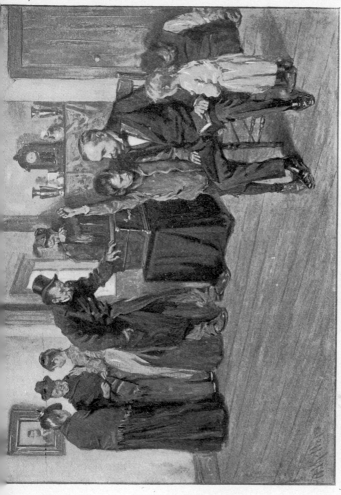

"I'll never touch it !"

FUNERAL OF A MOTHER DEAD FROM DRINK.

Little Jamie Kent makes a pledge, and Howard Russell decides his life-work.

the first Sunday evening in June—June 4, 1893—at a Union meeting of all the churches in the old First Church, Oberlin. Rev. Dr. James Brand, the pastor, at the opening of the service said among other things that he believed this would prove to be one of the great historic meetings in that church. He spoke of two such meetings already held. One, the Indignation Meeting with reference to the fugitive slave held by his captors in Wellington, which resulted in the rescuing party being sent from Oberlin to take him from them. Another when the two companies were recruited from faculty and students for the Civil War.

Dr. Brand said he believed a movement was to be advocated, and begun that night, which would be far-reaching in its influence against a most stupendous and satanic evil in the State and nation. He believed, he said, that in Mr. Russell they saw and were to hear "a man sent from God" for a definite work, who was now

about to set in upon his Heaven-ordained
task. He called upon all to both hear and
then act with reference to the important
plans to be presented. Professor G. W.
Shurtleff introduced Mr. Russell. He referred to the important work Mr. Russell
had already done for the people of Ohio in
managing the campaign in 1888, which had
secured the enactment of the Township
Local Option Law. He expressed his confident belief that with the wise and timely
plans which Mr. Russell had presented to
the Alliance and was now about to advocate
to the people, it would be possible under his
leadership to develop a permanent and
powerful organization aganst the liquor
traffic in Ohio. It was a wonderful meeting. The church was filled to overflowing;
students in the great galleries and earnest
and attentive listeners in all parts of the
house.

Mr. Russell, in his speech that night,
called attention to the fact that the saloons
were increasing three times as fast as the

population, and showed the need of a more
powerful organization than then existed in
Ohio to antagonize the liquor traffic. He
insisted that the churches ought to become
responsible for a vigorous and permanent
anti-liquor league. He advocated an omni-
partisan and interdenominational federation, which should overcome the apathy,
cowardice, and discord then existing among
temperance people, and under the leadership of at least ten competent men,
employed as experts, to devote their whole
time to the work should carry forward
a permanent campaign on four distinct
lines: first, Agitation; second, Legislation,
third, Law Enforcement; and, fourth, An
Organization of the Boys. At the close of
his speech he appealed for liberal subscrip-
tions to support the movement. Printed
three-year pledges were circulated and the
aggregate sum pledged was over $600 per
year for three years or nearly two thousand
dollars. A private canvass soon increased
the subscription to three thousand dollars,

and it is an interesting fact that Oberlin, that grand old reform center, with no saloons, and the law well enforced, has given about one thousand dollars per year during the past ten years through the treasury of the Anti-Saloon League, to do missionary work for Ohio and the country in the cause of temperance.

The Ohio Anti-Saloon League was born that Sunday night in the church in Oberlin. It soon spread over the State and the bold prediction of its founder, that the people of the churches would form a mighty league against the saloons, was soon fulfilled. Russell was tireless in service and abundant in success. He soon interested men who had both conscience and capital to devote to the cause. Two of them deserve special mention. They are the late E. W. Metcalf of Elyria, and Mr. A. I. Root of Medina, Ohio. These men by their counsel and generosity helped give the new venture a rapid start. The League was soon felt in legislation; bad legislation was stopped,

and advance measures were taken; laws
long disused and disobeyed were brought to
light and enforced, until the eyes of temperance people all over the nation were attracted to the Ohio idea of aggressive concentration against the saloon.

In 1894 and 1895 Russell began to have
many calls from the outside for information
about the Ohio Anti-Saloon League and its
work.

Neighboring States began to organize
along the same lines. A call for an Inter-
state Convention for four or five of the
interior States, with a view to forming an
Inter-State Anti-Saloon League, had been
prepared, and was about to be issued, when
a letter came from the Anti-Saloon League
of the District of Columbia inviting the
Ohio Anti-Saloon League to join in a call
for a convention to organize a National
Anti-Saloon League. The Ohio Anti-
Saloon League joined in that call and the
American Anti-Saloon League was formed
at Washington in December, 1895.

The immediate origin of the National
Anti-Saloon League may be properly said
to have come from four distinct sources. In
the first place there had been non-partisan
State temperance organizations at work for
several years previous to the organization
of the Anti-Saloon League. These were the
Total Abstinence Society in Massachusetts,
the Connecticut Temperance Union in Connecticut, the Kansas Temperance Union in
Kansas, and the Maryland State Temperance Alliance in Maryland. At least three
of these old State organizations took part in
the convention at Washington in 1895
which organized the American Anti-Saloon
League, and they have all since as bodies,
federated with the National organization.
In the second place a movement had been
planned and carried forward by the Rev.
Dr. A. J. Kynett in connection with his
regular work as Secretary of the Church
Extension Society of the Methodist Episcopal Church. Dr. Kynett called the
organization which he furthered the Inter-

denominational Christian Temperance Alliance. He printed a monthly magazine in connection with his Church Extension Society work, and this magazine contained a department relating to saloon suppression, in which he advocated the organization of branch Alliances in the different localities throughout the country, and as far as such branches were organized he reported their work in that department of the magazine. He advocated the forming of organizations in each local Methodist church and urged that the churches of other denominations should form like organizations and seek alliance with each other in the various localities and States. To some extent he had succeeded in securing such church and local organizations, and in three States, Pennsylvania, Illinois and Ohio, conventions had been held and officers elected to inaugurate State organizations along the same lines. Not a great deal of work had been done through these organizations, as Dr. Kynett himself stated, for lack of a

Superintendent who could devote his whole
time to the organization and direction of
the movement. Dr. Kynett was glad to
join forces with the new movement planned
at the Washington Convention, and he was,
during the early years of the American
Anti-Saloon League, one of its most wise
and faithful counselors and leaders. The
third source of the Anti-Saloon League
movement was found in the federation of
the churches and temperance societies in
the District of Columbia which was formed
June 23, 1893, under the name of the District of Columbia Anti-Saloon League, and
which had already at the time of the convention in 1895, done very useful service
for the temperance cause at the Capital.
Among those who were influential in the
District of Columbia League when the National League was formed, may be mentioned Mr. A. N. Canfield, who had called
the first conference looking toward the federation of the Churches and Temperance
Societies of the District of Columbia

in an Anti-Saloon League, and Mr. James
L. Ewin, who was the first secretary
of the National Organization, and is its
present corresponding secretary, and who
has devoted much time and self-sacrificing
service in connection with the calling and
management of the various conventions of
the League at Washington, and in the fur-
therance of the League's growth. Rev.
Luther B. Wilson, D. D., a presiding elder
of the M. E. Church at Washington, was
more than any other man influential in
causing the call for a National Organization
to be issued. He was at that time President
of the District of Columbia League, and was
elected First Vice-President of the National
League. After the death of the Hon. Hiram
Price, who was the first President of the
National League, Dr. Wilson was elected
to succeed him as the League's President,
and he has been a most able presiding
officer. The fourth source of influence in
the forming of the National League is
found in the Ohio Anti-Saloon League

with its successful history of organization and achievement prior to the Convention at Washington in December, 1895, to which it sent its delegates to take part in the forming of the National organization. Back of or contemporaneous with all these four lines of influence which have been named, were the organized efforts made by temperance workers in all parts of the United States, which had resulted in the agitation of the temperance question and the concreting of the public sentiment thus engendered into statute law, and the obtaining of the enforcement of the law in the various localities throughout the country. The organizing Convention adopted a Constitution providing for a federation of all organizations pledging co-operation in the suppression of the saloon.

The object of the League as stated in Article Third is as follows: " The object of this League is THE SUPPRESSION OF THE SALOON. To this end we invite the alliance of all who are in harmony with this object,

and the League pledges itself to avoid af-
filiation with any political party as such,
and to maintain an attitude of neutrality
upon questions of public policy not directly
and immediately concerned with the traffic
in strong drink."

An Executive Committee was elected in
harmony with the Constitution, and provision was made for future annual conventions of the National League. These
Conventions have been held with an increasing attendance and a growing federation of organizations to promote the objects
of the League. The National Organization
now federates about 250 church, temperance, and other bodies in all parts of the
country. The Ohio Anti-Saloon League was
recognized as the "model" for other State
Leagues to be formed throughout the country, and the Superintendent of the Ohio
League was elected the first Superintendent
of the National Organization. Gradually
the beginning of work has been promoted in
the various States since 1895; in some cases

by correspondence, but with greater satis-
faction and success, by a visit to the new
State by the National Superintendent. In
1897 Superintendent Russell spent three
months introducing the work in California
and other States in the Far West. For two
years after the National League was formed
Superintendent Russell served as Superintendent both of the Ohio League and of the
National League, and during the years 1902
and 1903 he was Superintendent both of the
National League and of the New York
State Anti-Saloon League. During two of
the years of his superintendency he traveled
over 50,000 miles each year in connection
with the work of organization in new States
and the fostering of the work in the States
where the League had already been formed.

A bright judge of men and great human
movements says : " Successful leadership depends entirely upon one's ability to multiply
himself through others. Great leaders
must not only lay plans which are practical
but must also be able to call around them

those who can carry out their orders effi-
ciently and vigorously." This is one of
Howard Russell's personal qualities, and
has contributed greatly to his success as
Superintendent of the American Anti-
Saloon League.

Among many others whom he has chosen
and enlisted to co-operate in the expansion
of the League, a few names may be mentioned of those who have been longest
associated with the work. The Rev. E. C.
Dinwiddie, of Springfield, Ohio, was one of
the first men called. He was given special
charge of the legislative department of the
Ohio League, for which work he showed
great aptitude. After four years in Ohio
he took entire charge for two years of the
Pennsylvania League, and now for three
years has been at the National Headquarters
of the League in Washington, D. C., where
he is National Legislative Superintendent.
He is a man rarely qualified for such tasks,
and his work has met with gratifying success. The Rev. P. A. Baker, of Columbus,

Ohio, was first employed as a District Superintendent of the Ohio League, and was elected State Superintendent when Dr. Russell resigned to assume the duties of the Superintendency of the National League in 1897. Baker has carried forward and developed the League in that State with masterly ability and success. He is as brave as a lion, as wise as a serpent, and a man of remarkable adaptation to his position. In the expansion of both the State and National Leagues, Baker and Russell have been true yoke-fellows. They are the Cobden and Bright of this mighty movement for reform. Mr. Wayne B. Wheeler was one of the bright men of the class of 1895 in Oberlin College. Upon his graduation from college he began as a field secretary in the Ohio League, and later was admitted to the Ohio Bar, and has since made a brilliant record as attorney for the Ohio Anti-Saloon League. The Rev. Dr. J. C. Jackson was called from an important Columbus pastorate to the League work in 1896, and after assisting Superintendent Russell, both in the State League work, and in organizing new Leagues in other States, he was appointed editor of *The American Issue,* the organ of the Ohio League, and soon to be that of the National Organization. By his voice on Sunday, and his pen during the week, Dr. Jackson is exerting a mighty influence for the cause.

Time would fail to mention other names as worthy of record. One after another, strong men have been sought out and placed at the head of the various State Organizations, and in charge of the equally important district work in many of the States. A particular reference to these leaders and organizers must be omitted for lack of space, but they are exerting a powerful influence in molding public sentiment against the liquor traffic. Nor will it be possible further to recite the wonderful growth and spread of this marvelous movement. Suffice it to say that a little over ten years ago Dr. Russell, first privately, then publicly, at the great Oberlin meeting, proposed the League system of State-wide Anti-Saloon work as it has since been developed throughout the land. At that time, to quote Professor Whitlock, " he was the only salaried officer. Its headquarters were in his valise. Its stock in trade were his faith and heroism, and the sympathy and prayers of a few friends and advisers "; while to-day, according to Dr. Russell's last annual report, there are thirty-nine States and Territories in which organization has been started, wherein over two hundred and fifty persons are devoting their entire time to the work, and the financial support for the year in the various States and in the National League will approximate a quarter of a million dollars.

THE LINCOLN LEGION

Whereas, the use of alcoholic liquors as a beverage is productive of pauperism, degradation and crime, and believing it is our duty to discourage that which produces more evil than good, we therefore pledge ourselves to abstain from the use of intoxicating liquors as a beverage.—The pledge signed and advocated by Abraham Lincoln.

CHAPTER XI

THE LINCOLN LEGION

THE history of the Temperance Reformation will show very clearly that the great cause of sobriety, as well as the enactment and enforcement of laws prohibiting or restricting the liquor traffic, has made the most rapid progress at such times as there have been general movements toward what is known as " moral suasion " methods. In the very nature of things, agitation, persuasion, appeal, arouse public sentiment against the liquor habit and the liquor traffic, and these, after all, must be depended upon as the great sources of prohibitory law and enforcement.

What an awakening of conscience, and what a change in the views and habits of the people of the whole country during the Father Matthew, the Washingtonian, and the Murphy campaigns! The fact that a drinking man was battling against his appetite and inducing others to likewise enter the conflict, made John B. Gough an influential leader of thought, and by his life and words the liquor traffic was greatly weakened throughout the land. The open doors of immigration have admitted millions of people whose past habits have included the use of alcoholic beverages. The turning of attention by the leaders of the temperance reform in recent years to an almost exclusive contest against the place of sale of liquor, and the general neglect of the popular appeal for personal abstinence has, in many localities, pressed the reform disproportionately upon the legal side. It is a fact that in those localities where a large enough ratio of the people are abstainers from the habit, there is no difficulty in obtaining the legal abolition of the traffic in alcoholic drinks. There are many hopeful signs that from a business standpoint social liquor drinking is becoming unpopular.

The railways and many other industries are discouraging and prohibiting the use of alcoholics by employees. To be in the habit of drinking is a detriment to any man seeking any kind of employment—even that of a bartender.

This hopeful sign in the business world does not, however, obtain in modern society. There the aspect is alarming, and, not only in what is known as the " Four Hundred," but among the great middle-classes of well-to-do people in the large towns and cities of America, there is in many circles an alarming increase in social drinking. The writer has conversed with many distinguished clergymen of the leading denominations, during the last two or three years, on this subject, and he is assured by pastors of great churches that at weddings, and social receptions held in the homes of the wealthy members, in families that for a generation, have been practicing total abstinence, the punch-bowl is now coming in, and alongside the bowl of lemonade, there is the one of wine, and that the wine is patronized by the church people to an alarming extent. But, to my mind, the most serious phase of the situation to-day is the undoubted increase in the drinking habit of respectable well-to-do women. The writer frequently meets it in his pastoral work, and every pastor in the great cities is constantly coming in contact with the ruin that is being wrought through the drunken woman. Women order "cocktails" in the public restaurants without question in some of our large cities, and these are not lewd women, but are frequently women who are members of leading Protestant churches. Surely it is high time to call a halt. It is time that the trumpet is sounded for a new movement for total abstinence and safety. The great danger belt in the temperance movement lies in the army of moderate drinkers. While the greatest tolerance and the kindliest spirit should ever be used in dealing with those whose past training and environment have made them in favor of the so-called moderate use of liquor, it is undoubtedly the supreme duty of the churches and all moral people who see the peril of the habit, to cry out in warning.

A subtle sophistry, which is very widespread, more widely than the casual observer knows, needs to be overthrown. This is the belief among laboring people that an alcoholic stimulant is necessary to the working man. If it is not thought essential, it is at least believed to be very strengthening and helpful. It is of great importance that the truth to the contrary be attractively and persistently taught upon this question.

Why is it that Gospel temperance and pledge-signing urges forward so effectively the whole reform? The reason is this: Pledge-signing meetings arouse attention to the perils and waste of the drink habit. They put the whole community on inquiry and compel personal decisions; they awaken judgment and conscience, both as to habit and traffic. If alcohol is harmful as a beverage, and causes crime, poverty, and disease, then the abolition of its retail sale in the community is logically in order. So a gospel temperance campaign is a flank movement against the saloon. As an impetus to real revivals of religion, the temperance campaigns have been a marked blessing. It needs no analysis to see the reason for this. The moral sense of the whole citizenship is awakened by a series of gospel temperance services, and it is easy to go forward with the preaching of the pure gospel of salvation from all sin by the power of a personal Saviour. Many a minister living to-day can testify to the good agency of a temperance campaign as leading to a religious revival. Do we not need to-day such a moral awakening as we should have just reason to expect from a general movement for total abstinence?

Personally, I do not believe that there will be any great general revival of religion in the United States until the church generally becomes aggressive on the subject of the liquor traffic. We may issue all the mani-

First public meeting of the Ohio Anti-Saloon
League held here, June 4, 1893.

Chapel where State League was
formed, September 5, 1893.

THE OLD "FIRST CHURCH," OBERLIN.

Birthplace of the Ohio Anti-Saloon League.

festos we please, and declare that this or
that year is to see a great revival. But it
will not come to pass until the church re-
pents of its indifference towards the hundreds of thousands of God's weak children,
who are being ruined and destroyed through
the oppressions of the liquor traffic. It is
because I believe, with all my heart, that the
best way to arouse the church to adequate
activity on this momentous question is to
return to first principles, and awaken the
conscience of the people anew to the sin of
drunkenness, to the duty of brotherly influence, and to a keen sense of brotherly
obligation, as well as to the enormity of the
crime of selling liquor, that the author, a
Christian minister, and a Prohibitionist,
urges with hopeful and devoted enthusiasm
this new pledge movement, the Lincoln
Legion.

After long study of the situation, Dr.
Howard Russell decided to sound a number
of leading comrades in temperance work to
see whether they would agree with him that

the hour was ripe for carrying forward systematic pledge-signing enrollment throughout the whole country in connection with the churches, which should include substantially the features which have been embodied in the Lincoln Legion.

The responses received from several hundred pastors and temperance workers throughout the land have been favorable and generally enthusiastic in their endorsement of these propositions submitted by Dr. Russell. We can quote only a few of them here. These are typical statements:

Rev. Francis E. Clark, D. D., of Boston: " I like your plan, and believe it is along the right line."

Bishop Samuel Fallows, Chicago: " I will do all in my power to advance the work so important and far-reaching that you are undertaking."

Rev. Albert G. Lawson, D. D., Camden, N. J.: " It is wise and timely. Much of our present weakness has come from just such neglect of moral and Christian effort as you propose."

Rev. S. S. Scovill, D. D., Wooster, Ohio: " It is a movement in the right direction."

Mrs. Mary H. Hunt, Boston: " I heartily approve, if accompanied by education as to the nature and power for evil of alcoholic drinks."

Rev. James D. Hill, D. D., Salem, Mass.: " I have the clear opinion that we ought to do no less to shut up saloons, but ought to do more to get men to stop drinking. When men stop drinking the saloon will stop."

Rev. W. H. Hickman, D. D., Greencastle, Ind.: " The plan is good; will commit the people; certainly I endorse this movement."

Mrs. Ellen J. Phinney, Cleveland, Ohio: " I do approve most heartily. We can enroll a mighty host."

Rev. A. Z. Conrad, D. D., Worcester, Mass: " It is the great need of the hour. It will educate and stimulate. It will give the saloon a blow between the eyes."

William Shaw, Boston (Treasurer C. E.

Society) : " It is fundamental. Political prohibition is helpless without it."

John Sobieski, Neosho, Mo.: " I think it just the thing. Will do all I can to push it."

President W. O. Thompson, D. D., Columbus, Ohio: " Heartily in favor; something must be done to arouse the younger element of society to its danger."

Rev. P. S. Henson, D. D., Chicago (now Brooklyn) : " I hail it as the hopefulest thing yet attempted. The practical, personal pledge has been too long neglected, for fireworks shot in the air and hitting nothing."

The National Executive Committee of the Anti-Saloon League some time since endorsed the plans submitted to them by Superintendent Russell, and approved the initiation of this movement. The State Board of Trustees of the New York State Anti-Saloon League, in June, 1902, did likewise. The League officers in several other States have given their sanction. The pastors of a number of important churches and many influential business men have promised their hearty co-operation. Everything augurs a hopeful and successful inauguration of this important work.

I have now told the story of the Lincoln Legion, its founder, and the persons and events which have anticipated and suggested this new movement. I wish to testify to my deep and growing interest in the coming Lincoln Legion. The times are opportune, the leadership will be masterful, the constituency will be enthusiastic.

As to the methods, as you read the prospectus which now follows, prepared by Superintendent Howard Russell, I am sure you will agree with me that a most attractive and workable plan of fellowship is offered by the "Lincoln Legion." It only remains for all who approve the purposes of the Legion to take a share in the sacrifice and service involved, and together we shall make the cause triumphant. "Fall in, and forward march!"

The Prospectus is as follows:

PROSPECTUS OF THE LINCOLN LEGION.

It is hereby proposed:

First, NAME: That we accept the inspiration of the life and teaching of Abraham Lincoln upon the question of Abstinence from Intoxicants; that we recognize his temperate example as a model for our practice, and that we honor his sacred memory by organizing a host of pledged abstainers to bear his name, and to be called THE LINCOLN LEGION.

Second, PLEDGE: That we make our pledge simple and brief in form and elastic as to time. Twelve words will be sufficient to embody the central organic idea which we place upon our banner:

"WITH GOD'S HELP,
I WILL ABSTAIN FROM ALL
INTOXICATING LIQUORS
AS BEVERAGES."

A choice is to be given the recruit in this Legion of three kinds of pledges as to time.

The Red pledge is a term pledge which binds the signer for a limited term; the length of which he states upon the pledge. This pledge is renewable, and it is the duty of the officers to see that it is renewed.

The White pledge is the life pledge, which will be ordinarily taken by those who are entirely settled upon the question.

The Blue pledge is for the children, limited to their reaching twenty-one years of age. Renewable for life, after reaching fifteen years of age.

Third, COLORS: The colors for a Lincoln Movement would naturally be our national colors. We have already had a Blue Ribbon and Red Ribbon Movement, while the White Ribbon of the W. C. T. U. has been everywhere a badge of abstinence. As we need in order to be successful, a unification of the efforts of all upon this work, so let us combine all our former emblems and in unison sing: " Three cheers for the red, white, and blue!"

Fourth, ENROLLMENT AND OVERSIGHT: It should be understood that the Lincoln Legion is to be built up by present organizations, thus unitedly promoting total abstinence. A new independent organization is not necessary nor desirable. A very simple form of administration is proposed, full details of which will be printed in a small handbook. The Legion will be subdivided into Hundreds, Thousands, County Divisions, and State Divisions. Suitable officers will be appointed, as for example, the Captain and nine Comrades in each Hundred and a Marshal and ten Captains in each Thousand. A County, State, and National President will be the leading officer of those respective Divisions of the Legion.

Fifth, INITIAL SERVICES AND REUNIONS will be held by the various subdivisions, at such times as may be agreed upon.

It is proposed that Lincoln's Birthday

shall be fittingly honored in every locality by this organization, which his marked sobriety and gracious memory have inspired, and that the Lincoln Legion shall do its part to redeem the Fourth of July from the empty clamor, and indifferent or objectionable observance, which have come to characterize too often the recurrence of our national holiday.

Sixth, AS TO CONSTITUENTS: The Lincoln Legion is to be an open society with no grips nor passwords, and is to be made up of men, women, young people, and children. It is hoped that it will become the practice for whole families to unite together as members of the same Hundred. All political partisanship is to be kept out of the organization, each member being free as to his party preferences.

Seventh, THE LEAGUE AND THE LEGION: With reference to the relationship of the LINCOLN LEGION to the Anti-Saloon League, the Legion may very conveniently be promoted by the League officers, since the League

is the direct agency of the churches, in which
especially the Legion must become strong if
it makes any headway and history for the
cause of Abstinence. While the Anti-
Saloon League will introduce and foster the
LINCOLN LEGION in many of the States, the
League will, however, claim no monopoly of
the work of organizing and promoting the
Legion. It is expected that any other
organization and any individual anywhere
may lend a hand in pushing forward the
good work of the Legion. The Legion will
support the measures of the League so
far as such measures appeal to the members
of the Legion as lines of activity which may
consistently be carried forward. It is reasonable to expect that the Legion will stand
for advancing legislation against the saloon
and that as an organization it will assist
in supporting public officials who will enact
and enforce reasonable temperance legislation in accord with general public sentiment. It is expected that in all the Reunions of the Legion will be discussed the

questions at issue with the Saloon in the State and community and that all possible efforts will be made to weaken the places of temptation to drink, so far as consistent with the non-partisan character of the Legion. A State Division Reunion, held annually or bi-annually, and largely attended, as it probably would be, would exert a powerful influence in advancing all phases of the reform throughout the State. As the League enlists those who are not total abstainers in its efforts to suppress the saloon, so the Legion will recruit and enroll as abstainers those who are willing to forego the practice of using liquor as a beverage, even though they be unwilling personally to enter upon aggressive work against the liquor traffic.

Eighth, As to the Expenses of the Legion: Each Hundred in adopting its bylaws will prescribe as it chooses as to its financial plans. The work will not be costly. It will be promoted largely by organizations already existing. Its Reunions will be held in the churches and other buildings which become responsible as posts for the work. The sums needed for literature and to send delegates to the Division and Legion Reunions may easily be raised by an offering at a regular Reunion of the Hundred or Thousand.

The Anti-Saloon League will provide all the printed matter necessary for recruiting and mustering the Hundred, and it is expected that the expenses of maintaining the State Division headquarters can be readily provided by an annual free-will collection by those Hundreds willing to take it up for that purpose. It is therefore thought best to prescribe no financial obligation, but to leave each member of the Legion free to do much or little or make no gift at all as he may freely choose to do in that regard.

Ninth, BADGES, BUTTONS, ETC.: It will deepen the interest and help spread the movement to have attractive badges, buttons, and insignia. These will come naturally as the movement develops. The Liberty Bell is suggested as one of the badges. The log house and the rails will be suggestive of Lincoln's early and honest struggles, and his benign face will be always suggestive of what we seek to teach and practice in the LINCOLN LEGION.

Tenth, THE SPIRIT OF THE LEGION: The most important point connected with the movement is the spirit which is to characterize it. If it is God-ordained, it will be Christlike in its aims and works. It will be inspired from the beginning with the spirit of true love. The 13th of 1st Corinthians will be the chapter embodying its high sentiments of tolerance and forbearance. With " Love " as its first watchword it will be easy to take up the burden of sacrifice which abstinence for the sake of others may require. It is often as useful to go without for the sake of the good of others as to do some positive act of helpfulness. So " Sacrifice " will be another important watchword. The LINCOLN

LEGION if it succeeds in doing the work anticipated by those who have thought intently and prayed earnestly at its beginning will have the spirit of the Helping Hand. The children are to be guided aright by example and precept and lovingly saved from beginning the perilous and wasteful habit of drink. The work of the Legion will not perform its anticipated duty unless it reaches an arm of help and salvation to multitudes who are overthrown and bound by the power of appetite for drink. As this is the most supreme need of this reform so it will be the most consecrated work of the Legion. Let its climax watchword then be " Service."

" LOVE, SACRIFICE, SERVICE! " The banner with such a motto leads the united disciples of Jesus Christ, inevitably, into the realm of evangelistic service. Is it too much to expect, through the Lincoln Legion, the turning from all sin by great multitudes of people? Grant this, O Almighty God!

Who can measure the vast possibilities of

such a unity in moral effort as is proposed in the LINCOLN LEGION? It means a quickening of the pace of a great reform. It means for many, salvation from present distress and dishonor. It means the opening of the Heavens with revival rains! If only we can catch anew the bright and glorious spirit of our honored leader, Abraham Lincoln! His was a life of Love, Sacrifice, and Service, inspired by the matchless Master, who "came not to be ministered unto but to minister, and to give His life a ransom for many!" In this spirit we summon forth into life and action, the hosts of

THE LINCOLN LEGION!

INDEX OF PERSONS AND FACTS REFERRED TO